Unstuck in Provence

The courage to start over

Unstuck in Provence

The courage to start over

CAROLYN TATE

Dedications

To my mother Joy, who taught me courage.

To my son Billy, who was courageous enough to take the journey with me.

Contents

Introduction	1
Prologue	7
1 Getting Unstuck	11
2 Bonjour Paris	63
3 Our New Home	90
4 Our Italian Adventure	193
5 Back in Aix	217
6 Beginning of the End	259
Epilogue	312

About Carolyn

Carolyn Tate is a businesswoman, mother, author, speaker and intrepid traveller. Apart from this book, she's written two marketing books – *Small Business Big Brand* and *Marketing your Small Business for Dummies*.

In 2010, she sold her house in Sydney, gave away most of her belongings, put her flagging business on hold, ended a highly unsatisfactory love affair and escaped with her 12-year-old son Billy, for an extended sojourn in the south of France. This is where she wrote the first draft of this book.

After returning to live in Melbourne with Billy in 2011, Carolyn worked with a women's not-for-profit for 12 months before reinventing her business from the ground up. Now she works with people she loves, on projects she loves, writing books, travelling, blogging, speaking and helping her clients reinvent their business too.

Carolyn passionately advocates for massive gender realignment and true equality for women everywhere, which is ultimately the real reason this book had to see the light of day.

To find out more about the book and Carolyn visit unstuckinprovence.com and carolyntate.co

Thank you

There are simply too many beautiful people to thank for supporting me in getting this book out into the public domain. There are all the wonderful, beautiful friends we made in France that feature in the book, and the many friends and family members back home who have given me the courage to publish it. You all know who you are.

In particular, I'd like to thank Billy's father, his step-mum, my mother, Joy, my sisters, Angela and Dianne, my friends Grace, Julie and Anna, my editor, Lucy, and my publisher, Julie.

Then finally, of course, there's Billy. This book was only made possible because of his courage to join me on the journey and his willingness to have his story told. I thank him for being so adept at scrutinising all parts of the book that featured him and offering his insightful edits. I also thank him for his wit, wisdom and love, as always.

Introduction – About this book

"Our lives begin to end the day that we become silent about things that matter." – *Martin Luther King Jr*

When we first went to live in Aix en Provence, I had another book in my head and a brilliant plan to write it there. It was *Real Women*, a book featuring the stories of nine extraordinary women who'd overcome major adversities in their lives.

Each of these women had deeply inspired me, and in their own way, were the catalyst for me to muster up enough courage to get unstuck from my own adversities.

Being an author of business books and never having written a book about the lives of women, I was frankly quite unprepared for how difficult the task would be. However, I did know it was going to be a highly emotional and intimate experience, and one that would require a great deal of compassion and creativity.

So with that in mind, I decided to accompany my writing with *The Artist's Way* – a book by Julia Cameron designed to unlock the latent creativity and talent in every person, whether that's writing, drawing, painting, singing, dancing or whatever. The 'morning pages' are the key to this program – three pages of freehand journalling to be done every single morning upon waking, with no filtering and no judgement.

For many years I'd tried to instil the discipline of meditation in my daily life with no success. My morning pages became my meditation.

At night I'd pose myself a question as I went to sleep, and then awake the next morning to discover the answer in my morning pages.

Even when I woke up feeling churlish, depressed or lonely, I'd still be looking forward to writing them.

The first two weeks of following *The Artist's Way* were filled with self-doubt about my ability to write *Real Women*. I'd been seriously procrastinating – which is easy when you've just arrived to live in a new country – and I couldn't seem to get my head or, more importantly, my heart, into it.

So one night in bed, just before I flicked off the light switch to go to sleep, I posed myself that all-important question – *Should I be writing* Real Women *or should I be writing a book about my own journey?*

And the morning pages answered clearly. *Write about your own journey and this time in France. Capture this experience while you're having it. It's essential for your healing and eventually it will help other women too.*

And so here you are now, not reading *Real Women* but *Unstuck in Provence*, my personal diary on how I got unstuck from a life that wasn't serving me and created a whole new life with my beautiful son Billy.

In the cold light of day, my own story seems insignificant compared to the stories of the millions of women around the world suffering under far worse conditions than I'll ever endure.

Introduction

I believe that the most pervasive and systematic human rights abuse occurring right now in the world is female genocide and gender inequality.

One in three women are subject to physical or sexual abuse in their lifetime.

Every week in Australia, one woman is killed by her partner.

Women account for 70% of the world's population living in absolute poverty on less than $1 a day.

One million women in the USA will be raped in the next 12 months.

In Australia, women earn 82c for every $1 a man earns. Globally women earn half of what men earn.

Only 4.5% of the Fortune 500 CEO positions are held by women.

An estimated four million women and girls are bought and sold worldwide each year, either into marriage, prostitution or slavery.

Clearly, over the last 2000 years, men have created a patriarchal system designed to benefit men. This system is the cause of the current level of insanity we now find our world in.

Sanity will only be restored through massive gender realignment and true equality, with the feminine traits of love, wisdom, compassion and humanity at the forefront of this revolution. The time for equality is now.

But this is not a women's issue. It's a human issue – one that can only be resolved in an inclusive way by women *and* men.

And the revolution must start with us women not being willing to accept this situation. It starts with each one of us releasing ourselves from our own personal bonds of slavery, in order to create lives of meaning and so that we can be of service to other women.

For every copy of *Unstuck in Provence* that's sold, I'll be donating 10% of net profits to The Hunger Project, a not-for-profit that puts women in developing countries at the centre of the process of bringing about equality in their community, and thereby solving their own hunger and poverty.

I hope my story resonates with you and inspires you to get unstuck – to shake off or wriggle out of the thing that may be preventing you from being the woman you were destined to be – because together we have much work to do!

Message from Cathy Burke
CEO Hunger Project Australia

The Hunger Project works to break the cycle of poverty, believing that hungry people themselves are the key to ending hunger. We believe that women should have roles working as equals to men, determining community priorities that transform lives.

In the mid 1990s I embarked on an investor leaders' field trip to Ethiopia with The Hunger Project. My guide on that trip was Lynne Twist, a co-founder and fundraiser with The Hunger Project USA and author of *The Soul of Money*.

From that first field trip, I knew that I'd found my vocation in life. I witnessed first hand the chronic hunger and malnutrition affecting a billion people, and how utterly unacceptable that was. I saw the top-down aid-driven charity models were failing to reach the people who needed the help. I became part of a different and sustainable approach to charity that empowered women to mobilise their community, identify their own solutions to hunger and move towards sustainable solutions.

Today, 20 years after that first field trip, I'm the CEO of The Hunger Project Australia. I'm extremely proud that globally we've mobilised and trained 400,000 local volunteer leaders who impact the health and rights of around 30 million people around the world.

I want to thank Carolyn for sharing our story along with hers, and for raising awareness and funds for the work that we do. To find out more about The Hunger Project and how you can get involved, visit thp.org.au.

Prologue

"There is a crack in everything. That's how the light gets in." – *Leonard Cohen, Anthem*

It was January 2000. I was 36. Out running my usual 10 kilometres, I'd sprinted around the final corner to face the big hill back home. I stopped to take a deep breath and prepare for my conquest.

Nothing. I couldn't move. I had zero energy. I wasn't going anywhere.

Instead, I sat in the gutter and broke down. Tears appeared from nowhere and turned into huge, heaving sobs.

I knew it right then and there – nothing would ever be the same again.

But what was the problem? I was a woman with a handsome husband, a beautiful two-year-old boy and a well-paying job at a big bank.

I was attractive, slim and smart. I had money, a beautiful home, a set of wheels and my independence. I also had a great family and great friends.

On paper, I had everything a woman could want. In reality, I didn't know who I was. On the outside I appeared happy and content. On the inside I felt numb and stuck.

I recall finally finding the energy to pull myself up out of the gutter and drag myself up the hill. With a heavy heart, I rehearsed the opening lines of the conversation with my husband I couldn't avoid any longer.

I don't recall the exact conversation, and I'd be doing him a grave injustice by sharing it here anyway, but needless to say it began an unavoidable chain of conversations that ultimately ended in separation and divorce – amicable but still painful.

That conversation also led to a new home, single-motherhood, financial self-sufficiency, an exit from the corporate world into my own business and a number of relationships that have taught me more about men (and myself) than I dare to recall.

It also led to some deep soul-searching and a quest to live a more spiritual life.

Ten years later, I find myself feeling stuck all over again. It's my second mid-life crisis and I'm only 46.

So what's my problem this time? If this spirituality stuff is so brilliant, how come my life isn't all peace and mung beans?

Well, in many ways it is. The past 10 years have been incredible fun. I've been true to myself and followed my passions. I've become an avid writer, producing two books. I've managed to eke out a living for myself and work flexible hours so that I'd be available for my son. I've travelled far and wide, cultivated many new friendships and connected with creative beings and entrepreneurs from all corners of the globe.

I've had an array of eclectic lovers, developed a love of learning, music and books, acquired an unconventional and compassionate view of the world and introduced Billy to the potential of living a more expanded, creative life.

Prologue

It's been a rich, wholehearted life and one I'd live all over again in a flash.

But on the other side of this fabulously semi-bohemian life there's also been the relentlessness of running a business I'm no longer passionate about, travelling lots for work, cooking and cleaning, walking the dog, maintaining a home and garden, struggling with the finances and paying the mortgage, attempting to keep fit and maintain my friendships and an unhealthy love affair, all while trying to be an available and loving mother to Billy. Phew!

It's been bloody tough being a single mum and not having a partner to share in the day-to-day burdens and joys of life, and the last couple of years have taken their toll. I'm exhausted and overwhelmed and I've been constantly asking myself, 'Is this all there is to life?' I feel like a clapped-out old racehorse that's been forced to run the same racetrack over and over again. I'm unhappy and stuck and I need to escape.

1
Getting Unstuck
Sydney to Melbourne Australia

Monday 17 May

SYDNEY, AUSTRALIA

"The only real valuable thing is intuition."
– *Albert Einstein*

It's 6.15am. I'm in that blissful sleepy state, drifting in and out of consciousness. I'm not yet aware of what hour or day it is. Dash, our cheeky black dog, is curled up on the end of my bed fast asleep. He knows he's not supposed to be there, but he's an opportunist and an optimist, like all dogs.

Often he wakes me with his licking and pawing, but not today. He's still snoring away like a warthog on his corner of my fresh white doona.

My blissful semi-conscious state is destroyed by a single conscious thought. I sit bolt upright in bed, fully awake. 'Let's move to Melbourne.'

For the first time in weeks, I'm up and ready for a run before Dash. As we head down the hill to the boardwalk along the cliff tops of Coogee, a million questions hit me.

Why Melbourne? Why now? Will Billy be happy about it? What will his dad think? What about his schooling? Will I sell our house or rent it out? What about Dash? Where will we live in Melbourne? What about my business? And… what about my dream of a French sojourn in 2011?

GETTING UNSTUCK

After 30 minutes of incessant self-questioning and very few answers, I plonk myself down on a huge boulder by the side of our favourite rock pool while Dash tentatively dips his paws in. I get comfortable, close my eyes and focus on my breathing. The only question that really needs answering right now is, 'Why?'

I listen for the answer.

'My son needs his father – who lives in Melbourne – to be in his daily life. And I feel stuck. I feel stuck financially. I feel stuck in a business I'm no longer passionate about. I feel stuck in a sad and painful love affair. I feel stuck in a monotonous daily routine. It hurts badly. I need to get unstuck – drastically.'

By the time Dash and I roll in the front door, my mind is made up. I don't have a single question still ringing in my head or tugging at my heart.

After dropping Billy safely off at his bus stop, I hurry home to take action before I lose my courage.

I grab my mobile and ring my ex-husband.

"What do you think of the idea of Billy and me moving to Melbourne?"

"Really?" He sounds astounded but happy. "I thought you loved Sydney and you'd never move."

"No, I'm keen for a change and I think our son needs you in his life more."

'Be careful what you wish for, Carolyn, because you just might get it,' I mutter to myself as we end the call.

Wednesday 19 May
Sydney

> "Solitude is painful when one is young, but delightful when one is more mature."
> – *Albert Einstein*

It's 10pm and I'm in bed exhausted. I've been burning the candle at both ends the last two days. I place my steaming cup of tea on a stack of books on my bedside table and stare at the ceiling. Something is seriously bothering me.

I cast my mind back to the glorious time I'd spent just last Christmas at a health retreat in Koh-Samui, cleansing my mind and body while Billy was spending the holiday with his father.

I've never really been a lover of the Christmas tradition and all the commercialism that goes with it, so it was a blissful escape into anonymity and isolation. Time on my own, a gift to myself. I was lounging in a hammock, gazing over the trees to the ocean and writing my bucket list, when the words 'France' leapt from my pen to the page.

And now that's what's seriously bothering me.

Before I'd decided on the move to Melbourne, the only thing that had kept me positive amid my feelings of being stuck was the possibility of going to France with Billy – soon.

But now there's no way it could happen – not soon enough,

anyway. I tell myself I can't have everything. Maybe France just wasn't meant to be.

I gulp down the last mouthful of tea and feel the disappointment in my gut. I flick off the light switch and pray my exhaustion will send me quickly into the land of nod.

⚜ ⚜ ⚜

Sydney

"Life is either a great adventure or nothing."
– Helen Keller

I'm sharing an early evening drink at my home with Billy's father and his wife.

As Billy is engrossed in some TV show, blissfully unaware his life is on the cusp of big change, we're quietly discussing the move to Melbourne. We agree on a few things quickly. Billy would start school in Melbourne in January 2011. We'd split the care arrangements 50/50. I'd sell my house and buy in Melbourne eventually, but in the meantime I would rent my ex-husband's new wife's townhouse from her. It all seemed very civil and very possible, if not a little weird.

And that's when the idea of France resurfaces. While two nights previously I'd all but killed that dream, I wasn't quite yet ready for it to die completely.

Billy's father had known about the France idea and had given it his blessing some time ago. Tentatively I raise the question.

"I'm not sure how – or if – our trip to France fits in with these plans… I guess we can't be going to France when Billy has just started a new school in Melbourne."

Billy's step-mum replies: "Have you thought about going in August this year? It's a nice time of year to go."

For a moment I'm speechless.

I quickly calculate how much time it would take to get unstuck from our Sydney life, move to Melbourne and be on a plane to France.

"That's three months. Plenty of time," I exclaim.

Has a woman ever been so full of love for an ex-husband's new wife? I think not.

Getting Unstuck

Friday 28 May

SYDNEY

> "When two people decide to get a divorce, it isn't a sign that they don't understand each other, it's a sign that at last they have begun to." – *Helen Rowland*

I'm sitting with Billy and his father, roast dinner on the table, a glass full of cabernet merlot and Dash salivating at my heels with a hungry look in his huge black eyes. We eat and chat about the week, but I can hardly taste the food. The small talk we're having is the warm-up for the big talk we're about to have with Billy.

I look at my ex-husband. I'm grateful that we've maintained a friendship and respect for each other and that our love for Billy has always been greater than the pain of our broken marriage. We've never been to lawyers, we've rarely argued, and we've given each other the grace and space to follow our own paths. But most importantly, we've put our son first.

My lawyer-loving divorced friends tell me I'm lucky to have such an amicable relationship. Yet I know it has nothing to do with luck. We've worked hard at it and I'm very proud of how we've managed the relationship.

I take a long sip of wine and a deep breath before I face Billy. He knows something is up.

"How would you feel about us moving to Melbourne to live in January, after we take that trip to France we've been talking about?"

If I ever needed a moment of affirmation, this was it. His reaction astounds and delights both his dad and me.

"That's so cool. That's so cool. I can't believe it! When is it happening? Tell me the details."

It was clear to us both that he really wanted to spend more time with his dad.

It was like we'd taken a huge weight off his shoulders. Now he'd never have to make a choice between living in Sydney or Melbourne. He'd have both parents and a great step-mum all in the one city.

Tears well up in my eyes at his reaction. I couldn't have imagined he'd be so willing to embrace this big change. And now my big, affectionate, warm-hearted, 6-foot-tall, 12-year-old son is crying too.

It's a small moment in the big scheme of things, but one I'll always remember.

Getting Unstuck

Tuesday 1 June
Sydney

"The time is always right to do what is right."
— Martin Luther King

A knock on the front door sets Dash barking and racing to find out who our visitor is. He greets the wary real estate agent like a long-lost friend, jumping up on the man's Armani trousers until I haul him off and banish him to the backyard.

I'm about to sign the papers to sell the house that's been our home for the last 10 years. I'm a little scared. Am I doing the right thing? Is it the right time to sell? Should I just rent it out until I find my next place? And, of course, will I get the price I want? All very practical and rational questions.

So I throw rationality and practicality aside and try to feel – not think – my way through this decision. Frankly, the house has become a millstone around my neck. The mortgage doesn't seem to be getting any smaller and the whole place needs a serious facelift – one I don't have the patience, interest or cash for. I could never see myself living there again even if I did come back to Sydney. And most importantly, it just doesn't seem like keeping it is going to give me the freedom I'm craving. I need to cash up and move on. The house has to go.

I look over the papers and check the dates in my diary: Auction – 3 July… Settlement – 13 August… Melbourne – 14 August… France –23 August.

"Oh my God!"

I hug the agent.

"I can't believe I'm doing this!"

I sign the papers with a flourish of the pen and a big smile on my face and escort him to the front door. Funny, he's smiling too.

I grab a cup of coffee and sit on my balcony overlooking Coogee.

'Good decision.'

⚜ ⚜ ⚜

Friday 4 June
MELBOURNE

"Our actions are the result of our intentions and intelligence." – *E. Stanley Jones*

The plane skids to a halt. We're here to visit two possible schools for Billy.

As we disembark, the grey, freezing cold and depressing Melbourne weather hits us with full force. Doubt floods in

Getting Unstuck

with it. We've just left behind beautiful sunny Sydney with one of the most beautiful blue, glistening coastlines in Australia. Why the hell are we moving here?

I get over it and of course don't express my doubts to Billy.

Billy, his father and I are at the first school waiting in reception all dressed up like we're about to be interviewed for a job. After thorough scrutiny on both sides and a tour of the school, we're told there's only a very slim chance of a vacancy for next year but that Billy should come back for a test in the afternoon anyway.

We're all very disappointed. It seems like a fabulous school.

We head off to the next school. Same story. No vacancies. But we don't mind. We don't think the school is a fit for Billy anyway.

I'm silently starting to panic. If we can't get Billy into the school we want, all of our plans for Melbourne and France could go up in smoke. I'd have to take the house off the market and go back to being stuck – an option I'm not prepared to accept.

It's now 4pm and Billy has done the test. I'm in the hotel room attempting to take a nap when the phone rings – an unknown number flashes on the screen. It's the admissions officer from the school.

'Billy did well in his tests and we'd like to offer him a place in Year 8 next year.'

YES!

We're all ecstatic. I say a little prayer of thanks to whoever might be listening up there for helping us take one more step on our adventure.

We celebrate over dinner at what's going to be our new local pub and restaurant. It's groovy, rowdy, and cosy and serves delicious French fare. The grey, dirty weather that greeted us this morning is forgotten as I chow down on duck pie and think how wonderfully European Melbourne is and how much fun we'll have here.

⚜ ⚜ ⚜

Tuesday 8 June
SYDNEY

"In all things, it is better to hope than to despair."
– *Johann Wolfgang von Goethe*

It's late at night. I can hear Billy and Dash snoring in unison as I slouch at the kitchen table clearing up weeks of boring emails. At least I have Leonard Cohen and his soulful, beautiful poetry set to music to get me through it. When I've hit delete on the last email, I allow myself the luxury of a big bold red and a bit of planning for our French adventure.

I'd already set my heart on Aix en Provence as our main destination. I knew it had a gorgeous climate and was just 10 kilometres from the International Bilingual School of Provence where Billy could be taught in English and fast-tracked in French. I'd been to Aix some years earlier and remembered it as a lively city filled with markets, shops and restaurants, and with a friendly, intimate and happy vibe. So Aix (pronounced 'ex') literally marked the spot!

Many months ago, when the France idea first came about, I'd tentatively applied for Billy to attend the International Bi-Lingual School of Provence in January 2011 for a term. But now the rules were changing. I needed them to accept Billy for the first term of the new school year beginning 6 September 2010 – just three months away.

I draft a friendly, and hopefully convincing, email fuelled no doubt by the big bold red and ask them kindly to accommodate our change of date.

That's when I look at the date and my heart sinks. Would anyone even be answering emails when every school in France was on the verge of closing down for the long summer holidays?

I cross my fingers as I hit the send button. I've no idea what I'll do if I don't get a response or the answer is no. It feels like I'm being tested every step of the way.

Thursday 10 June
SYDNEY

"Dogs have a lot of love." – Steven Tyler

It's 6am and I'm in my pyjamas. I sneak a peak at my emails before I get ready for a walk. It's an annoying habit I've been trying to break, this checking of emails at all hours of the day and night. But there's just one email I'm desperate to receive. And there it is!

"We'd be delighted to accept Billy into Grade 8 at IBS of Provence for the first term of school commencing Monday 6 September."

Dash looks at me accusingly as I sit down at my desk instead of jumping into my walking gear.

"Sorry, you'll just have to wait," I tell him.

I review the dates. We'll arrive in Paris on 23 August then take the TGV to Aix en Provence on 1 September. That'll give us five days to settle in before Billy starts school on 6 September. Perfect!

I craft an email to my travel agent with our dates and hit send, jump into my walking gear and bounce out the door with Dash. He's a bit subdued and I'm worried he's starting to get a whiff that change is in the air. Is that possible?

Getting Unstuck

Friday 11 June
Sydney

"If it wasn't for dogs, some people would never go for a walk." – Unknown

Billy is fast asleep and it's still dark outside as I pull on my walking gear and shoes, and wrap a scarf around my neck. Dash is already waiting at the front door, ready to take me for a walk. I give him a big rub on the head and a cuddle before we plod down the hill to the dog park.

There'll always be some heartache in any big decision like ours. And the source of that future heartache is staring up at me with big black doe-like eyes, waiting for me to let him off the lead so he can escape into the bushes or rob some other poor unsuspecting dog of his ball.

With our impending life changes it's going to be nigh on impossible to give Dash the stable home environment he needs. I look fondly at him running around the park, making his mark, and decide I need to start looking for a new home for him immediately.

For the first time I feel completely selfish about the move. I find a secluded bench and have a little cry. After a while I pick myself up, call Dash and go back home to Billy. With love and care I get him ready for school, all the while carefully avoiding any talk of Dash. I know he'll be devastated at the decision, and I don't want to say anything until I've found the perfect home for our beautiful dog.

⚜ ⚜ ⚜

SYDNEY

"Reason is powerless in the expression of love."
– *Rumi*

I can see James across the dog park. Our eyes meet and my heartbeat quickens. For over three years, I've been spellbound by this man. While he's not the only reason for my desperate need to get unstuck, he's definitely a very big contributing factor.

I'd first met James at a friend's party and then got to know him a little at our local dog park while the dogs would play together. In the beginning there was no spark, just pleasant chitchat. He was not the kind of man I'd normally be attracted to.

Then one night he invited me for dinner at his place. It was a very pleasant evening, nothing romantic, just great company, lots of laughs, brilliant food and intelligent conversation. I also gained an insight into the life of a complicated and compassionate person who was unlike any other man I'd met.

Over the ensuing weeks we got to know each other. I found him both interesting and interested, and while not conventionally handsome, he was charming, eccentric and passionate, and we shared a love of music and books.

Before I knew it, I found myself in bed with him. Admittedly I'd been the one to initiate this liaison, although he was clearly very willing to participate. Then somehow the relationship turned into a highly passionate but private love affair.

James is a superb cook, a fabulous lover, a great listener and a sensuous and kind man who thinks nothing of dropping over with flowers, leaving a CD on my doorstep or taking care of Dash when I'm in need. He also introduced me to another great love of my life – Leonard Cohen.

When I'm with James, whether in person or just on the phone, time is of little consequence and I'm instantly able to forget about my day-to-day troubles. We laugh and talk about everything and nothing. At these times I feel happy, heard, loved and respected.

I've come to love James very much but some time ago I realised I wanted a different kind of relationship. I wanted a partnership – something he's never been prepared to offer me, which of course only makes me want him all the more.

James shows his unwillingness to change the status of our relationship in a million little ways. Often he won't return my texts or calls for days, if at all. After a wonderful evening together we'll go our separate ways the next morning, never sharing a breakfast out, a movie or even a simple relaxing day together. He's never introduced me to his friends or made our relationship public.

All this while I've been kidding myself that it's cool – that as a wilful, independent, semi-bohemian woman, a real partnership would only complicate my life anyway.

Many times I've tried to talk about this with James, but the words just get stuck in my throat and I end up acting invulnerable and invincible, intimating that I don't want anything more either for fear of losing what we have. I've accepted what I've been given and told myself that it's better to have something than nothing at all. James is also very good at keeping me hooked. Just when I'm ready to walk away, he throws the line out again and reels me back in.

The reality is, I've handed over my heart to a man who's elusive, noncommittal and frustratingly unattainable. I've conveniently ignored all the signs that he's unavailable to me and clung to the foolish notion that he really does love me, and that one day he'll simply wake up and want more.

In truth, I'm addicted to him. He's been impossible to give up, despite my many half-hearted attempts over the years. I've had zero capacity for mature womanly reasoning where James is concerned and it's cost me dearly.

It's cost me countless hours of wasted time spent obsessing over him, wondering where he is, what he's doing and why he's not with me. It's cost me the opportunity to create a loving partnership with someone who's actually available to me. And it's cost me my self-love and self-respect.

Now, we're standing close to each other in the dog park enjoying the experience of being connected again. Later over coffee he charms his way into my heart, yet again, before we go our separate ways home to work – where, as I attempt to write a detailed document with a serious deadline, I can't concentrate.

I'm unsettled to the point of total distraction. I can't get into my work and I'm overwhelmed by everything I have to do for this move. I'm like a petulant child and I need an escape.

Then, as if by magic, a text from James comes through. Four hours of bliss is the result.

⚜ ⚜ ⚜

Wednesday 23 June
SYDNEY

"No great marketing decisions have ever been made on quantitative data." – *John Scully*

It's 10am and I'm sitting across the dining table with my client Belinda, coffee in hand. We're coming up with creative strategies to market her business and increase her profits. I love this part of my business – the getting to know people, listening to their problems, ideas and fears, and helping them gain clarity.

At the end of the day Belinda leaves, excited about the future. I'm grateful she's trusted me to share her personal and business secrets. It's a privilege and refreshing to be thinking about someone else's challenges for a change.

I've been an author, speaker, trainer and consultant in the field of marketing for over 20 years, with 11 of those years in corporate marketing roles for the big banks and the last nine of them in my own business.

I admit, after Billy, my business has ruled my life. If I'm not working *in* it, I'm working *on* it, thinking about it, hatching plans on how to help my clients and how to make money.

While the business has served me well financially some years and not so well in others, the harsh reality is that I've lost the passion for marketing as a profession. While I love the people I get to connect with, I'm tired of the smoke and mirrors and manipulation of marketing and advertising generally.

With every other thing in my life being turned upside-down, maybe it's also time to turn my career upside-down? It would be fabulous not to work while I'm away so I can dream about my future livelihood without constraint. I seriously doubt I can afford the luxury, however.

So once Billy is in bed, I sit down and review my finances. I eliminate every unnecessary expense and prepare a detailed budget on what it will cost to live in France.

By the early hours of the morning I've calculated that our monthly expenses will be less than half of what it costs to live in Sydney. I make a bold decision that I'll allocate just enough money from the sale of the house to fund this trip so I won't need to work.

I tell myself to consider it an investment – in my future and my wellbeing.

The sense of freedom is overwhelming.

Monday 28 June
Sydney

"In a major matter, no details are small."
– Paul de Gondi

Billy and I are sitting in the reception of the French Embassy waiting for our number to be called. We're about to be interviewed for our Long Stay Visitor's Visa. Even getting this appointment had taken some fortitude.

It had also taken days of preparation and running around to organise the documentation. We needed application forms, police clearances, bank statements, a statutory declaration, proof of our accommodation in France and a letter from Billy's school confirming his enrolment.

I know how bureaucratic the French can be. If just one single document is missing or not 100 per cent correct and I have to make another appointment, it'd be touch and go.

Our number is called. We step up to the counter with documents in hand. I'm smiling broadly and being super pleasant. We're scrutinised, photographed and thumb-printed. I hand over each document one by one as they're requested. Tick. Tick. Tick. I'm growing more confident with each tick. We get to the end and the nice guy smiles, looks at me and says. "That all looks fine. Just one thing. Do you have permission from Billy's father to take him out of the country? We need a signed statement from him with his approval."

I gulp. There hadn't been anything on the forms anywhere requesting this and it hadn't even crossed my mind.

While I'm wondering fearfully what I should do, miraculously the guy stamps the documents 'processed' for despatch to the visa-processing centre.

"Don't worry," he says, "Send this authority form to Billy's dad, get him to complete it, sign it and fax it back to me ASAP, and I'll personally see that it gets processed. Have a nice day."

Hallelujah. Just one minor detail to fix and we'll be on our way.

Getting Unstuck

Saturday 3 July
Sydney

"Be like a duck. All calm on the surface, but paddling like the dickens underneath." – *Michael Caine*

It's now 10am – 15 minutes before the auction. I've been up since 5am getting the house in perfect condition, walking Dash and buying Champagne and croissants in anticipation of a celebration at 11am. I'm lucky it's a beautiful sunny day and the ocean, which can be seen from my back yard, is a shiny turquoise blue.

It'd been a tough week dealing with the agent. I'd been feeling a bit duped, actually. Of course, when he was touting for my business some weeks ago he'd been talking up the price, and then during the week he'd sent me an email outlining what he felt the four potential buyers would be likely to bid – all way below my line-in-the-sand price.

I wasn't going to let the agent control the outcome so I'd been on the phone day and night seeking advice from my dad, who is also a real estate agent. I'd learnt a lot about this shonky industry and how to play the game.

It's 10.45am and the agent and auctioneer are patiently waiting downstairs in the back yard with my friends, neighbours and the four parties supposedly serious about buying the property. I'm sitting upstairs with Billy and James waiting for the auction to start. In my hand is a small smooth gem, given to me by my friend Siemone. I'm turning it over and over in my hand. I'm grateful for something to keep me focused, grounded and resolute.

The auctioneer is talking up the property and opens the bidding. Nothing. A full five minutes passes before he forces the first bid. The bidding slowly takes off. Then it stalls. Then it starts again. It stalls again and two bidders drop out. The price is still substantially below the lowest amount I'll take.

The agent is nervous and keeps walking up and down the stairs to liaise between the auctioneer and me. He's trying to encourage me to let the auctioneer announce that the property is on the market. I summon up all my courage and tell him to ask the bidders to wait.

I retreat to my bedroom and call Dad for some moral support. He reminds me of my line-in-the-sand price and tells me to stick it out.

"When it gets to this price, it's on the market, and not before," I tell the agent. "Are you sure?" he asks. "I'm not sure we can get that much more."

"See what you can do," I say.

The real estate agent is sweating more than I am. He whispers my instructions to the auctioneer. I'm not even sure what the auctioneer says to the crowd, as his words are lost on the wind.

Amazingly, the bidding begins again. It stops well above my line-in-the-sand price. Thank God. It's over.

Getting Unstuck

Monday 5 July

Sydney

> "Man cannot discover new oceans unless he has the courage to lose sight of the shore." – *Andre Gide*

I'm on my way to see Grace who's been my counsellor and confidante for the past 18 months and has lovingly encouraged, guided and supported me in the process of these big changes.

I believe everyone should have a 'Grace' in their life – someone who's gone through significant healing themselves, who's qualified, independent and objective, who'll listen and not judge and give sound advice.

I like the spiritual approach Grace takes. She encourages my decision making to come from a point of compassion, love and faith. On the other hand, she used to be a lawyer, so is very capable of giving me a very direct dose of reality when I need it.

I know what I want to talk to her about today. Just weeks ago I was desperate to get unstuck. I was craving freedom. And now that I'm seriously on the path to getting it, I'm fearful. In just one month, I'll have no debt, no house, barely any belongings, no dog, no career, no man – or painful love affair, anyway.

And more importantly, I'll have seriously disrupted Billy's life and there'll be no going back.

Every anchor that was tying us to our old lives will have been hauled up and I'll be casting us both on an ocean with no land in sight. I'm just praying it won't be too rough and trust that Grace will give me some insights into how to navigate it.

I leave feeling at peace and knowing 100 per cent that I've made the right decision. Thank God for Grace!

⚜ ⚜ ⚜

Wednesday 7 July
Sydney

> "Some days you're the dog; some days you're the hydrant." – *Unknown*

Dash is in the back of the car. He's looking at me quizzically as if to say, 'This isn't the way to the dog park! Where are you going, woman?'

We're actually on our way to meet Maureen, Dash's potential new mum.

I know finding a home for him isn't going to be easy, because Dash certainly isn't the perfect dog. He's energetic and cheeky (okay, naughty). He steals other dogs' balls (but only if they're rubber), often won't come back when called, is a bit of an escape artist and generally does just what he wants.

While I'd like to blame it on his breeding (half beagle and half cocker-spaniel/poodle), I acknowledge that I've probably not been as diligent with his training as I should have. He's four years old and still acts like a naughty pup.

On the other hand, he's the most loving and playful dog you'll ever meet. He loves kids, adults and other dogs, and he's adaptable, intelligent, healthy and strong. In short, he's a dog with spunk.

He needs a family that'll love him despite his flaws and give him the strong hand he needs. So I've been sending emails to people, talking to dog lovers in the dog park, and generally talking Dash up as the perfect pet for the right family. I'm not even allowing myself to think about the options if we can't find a home he'll be happy in.

We knock on the door and Maureen answers with a warm welcome. It seems like love at first sight as Dash bounds in the front door and makes himself at home.

We spend a bit of time chatting and getting to know each other and make a plan for Dash to have weekend visits over the next month, to see if there's the potential for a long-term love affair. I really, really hope so.

Thursday 15 July

SYDNEY

*"On n'aime que ce qu'on ne possède pas tout entier.
We love only what we do not wholly possess."*
– Marcel Proust

I'm in bed. Not my own, but his. With James, of course.

I wonder yet again how I got here. I have no rational answer, for this has never been a rational love.

I shower, dress and wait for him in his kitchen. As I open the fridge door to refill my Champagne glass, an invitation stuck on the front stares me in the face… "To James and Sarah".

I feel physically sick. I'm trembling all over as every single lie I've ever told myself and every lie he's ever told me crash into this one single moment of harsh reality.

I'm staring at the invitation – a public declaration of his partnership with another woman that should've been me.

A white-hot feeling creeps up my neck as I hear him walking up the hall towards the kitchen. Holy hell, what do I do now?

I take a deep breath. He turns the corner into the kitchen, buttoning his shirt with a satisfied smile on his face.

"Who's Sarah?"

A look of tremendous guilt floods his face. We sit and he feebly explains he's been in a relationship (of sorts) with her since his last unhappy relationship had ended way before I'd even met him.

It's my turn.

"Why didn't you tell me this when we first met three years ago? Why didn't you just let me go then?"

I can hear myself pleading. I'm starting to feel completely numb all over.

"I did tell you," he says. "I sat across the desk from you in your office and told you I couldn't have a relationship with you."

I admit he did tell me that he couldn't have a relationship with me, but he didn't tell me why and there was definitely never any mention of Sarah.

I'd assumed it was just because he was still feeling the pain of his previous relationship and it certainly hadn't prevented us from continuing to see each other.

After what appears to be our very first honest conversation and with many tears on both sides, I stride out of his front gate and sob the whole way home.

At home, I slam the front door shut with a raging anger. I curse and scream and marvel at my stupidity. How can a 46-year-old-woman be so immature? How could I have not known he was in a relationship with someone else? Why didn't I have the courage to end our addictive dance years ago?

While I'm angry with him, I'm furious with myself for wasting so much time and energy on this man.

It's only 9pm. The bottle of wine in the fridge is beckoning me, ready to numb the pain and emptiness and be my friend for the next hour. Yet I know that wine will only ever be a temporary friend, with me one minute and gone the next, leaving me feeling emptier and sadder.

So, gathering together every skerrick of willpower I can muster, I don't open the fridge door – I kick it instead and go to bed.

They say the best way out is through, so that's what I'm going to do. I'm going to feel every inch of this betrayal and pain, cry it out and have faith that it will pass.

⚜ ⚜ ⚜

Friday 16 July
SYDNEY

"The greater your capacity to love, the greater your capacity to feel the pain." – Jennifer Aniston

The day is breaking and a beautiful warm ray of sunshine is streaming across my bed. I'm not yet fully awake until the events of last evening hit me with full force. I relive every single painful moment in my mind from start to finish. I remain perfectly still and do a mental scan of my body from the tip of my toes to the top of my scalp.

Is my body aching? No. Have I got a headache? No. Am I tired? Not too bad. It's amazing that I can feel physically okay after what happened. Then I do a check on my emotions?

Getting Unstuck

Am I still angry? Only a little. Am I sad? Yes, incredibly. Do I feel stupid and humiliated? Absolutely.

Yet there are other positive feelings creeping in and for a while they take over from the negative ones. Relief. Freedom. A sense of closure? The beginning of the end?

I know that James will be suffering too. He'll try to make contact and attempt to explain the situation and apologise.

I make a firm decision not to get furious at him when he does. With less than four weeks to go before we leave and so many other happy and exciting things to look forward to, I want to finish this entanglement with grace and dignity – as much as I can muster, anyway.

I've heard the best way to get over a broken heart is to physically distance one's self and then promptly get under someone else. Is France far enough and will I find a French lover to oblige?

⚜ ⚜ ⚜

Monday 19 July
SYDNEY

"Spiteful words can hurt your feelings, but silence breaks your heart." – *Unknown*

No word from James all weekend. I'm not really surprised. He no doubt spent it with Sarah. It physically hurts all over just to think about it.

An entire weekend of solitude in bed had been my only solace. Between the sheets, on my own, I'd been able to read, cry, read and cry some more.

It's a beautiful sunny blue-sky morning and I'm parked outside my favourite café grabbing a cup of coffee when I spot James on the other side of the road. I hope desperately that he hasn't spotted me too, and childishly scurry off around the corner to hide. I can't bear to see him right now, especially as I look like complete crap after a weekend of crying.

Too late. He sees my car with Dash barking happily at him inside. He comes looking for me and there's no escape.

"I've had the most awful weekend," he says. "I'm devastated about what's happened."

He appears so sad and sorry, and pleads for me to have coffee with him. I remind myself that this man is a master at throwing out the line and reeling it back in. A feeling of deep contempt takes over and I shove my free hand in my pocket for fear that it might turn into a weapon of mass destruction. I breathe deeply and compose myself.

"I can't really say much right now. I'm not sure if we have anything further to say. I'll let you know."

"I understand," he says, before ambling off sadly down the road.

Getting Unstuck

Wednesday 21 July
Sydney

"There's no disaster that can't become a blessing and no blessing that can't become a disaster."
– Richard Bach

I've relented. I'm sitting in a café waiting for James. I'm here, not because I'm expecting any miraculous declarations of love but because I want to understand why this situation has occurred and why, since the demise of my marriage, I'm so deeply attracted to unavailable and unsuitable men like James.

I'd first met Billy's father, my first love, at the tender age of 16 in high school and we'd been together for 20 years before we'd ended the marriage (the reasons for which won't be divulged here out of respect for him and Billy). Suffice it to say, the marriage had ended amicably and tenderly with our son being of prime importance to us both.

After entering into a committed relationship at such a young age, perhaps I've needed these unlikely liaisons to learn a lesson or two about love and to discover how to be truly content and happy, with and without a man in my life. I just hadn't anticipated that it would take me ten long years or more to learn the lesson!

It's not like there's been a long string of lovers, just a number of very different ones. There was the fun, cheeky, intelligent, globetrotting Irishman who I spent a week with before he had to go home, and who'd continually pop up again via email, text and phone.

Then there was the dope-smoking, David Lynch-movie-loving photographer with an awesome body who was my lover for a couple of years. During this time I also had a relatively short and intense relationship with a free-spirited, earthy, hippie-type masseur and naturopath who got scarily serious very quickly.

Then later there was another short relationship with a web developer and ex-pro surfer who had 10 surfboards and lived in a dingy little Bondi flat.

Oh, and there was the ex co-worker who was a bit of a vagrant and who appeared from time to time for drinks, dinner and fun, not to mention a guy I dated for a while who I discovered later was an escort with a penchant for cocaine (not sure how I went so horribly wrong there). Plus the other various dates, liaisons and flirtations that never turned into anything.

Then, just a year or so ago, during one of my various attempts to eliminate James from my life, I'd met a lovely man who could have potentially been the most suitable man for me, ever. He was strong, loyal, kind, honest, intelligent and capable of deep conversation and emotion. But one day, just four or five months into it, it was crystal clear to us both that our partnership didn't have a future. He was still suffering badly from the recent break-up of his marriage and being physically distanced from his children, and secretly I was still distracted by thoughts of James. When we parted, to get over my sadness, of course I turned to James again.

Getting Unstuck

There's an old saying that every person comes into your life for a reason, a season or a lifetime. Every one of these men had come into my life for a reason, a few for a season, but none were ever likely to remain for a lifetime.

I stop reminiscing about my past loves and an intriguing thought crosses my mind about James. Maybe our relationship was a blessing, not a curse? If he'd wanted something more, we may never have been moving to Melbourne or going to France. And very importantly, Billy may not have had this opportunity to spend more of his teenage years with his father.

James walks in the door and sits down as close as he can get to me and reaches for my hand. I remember Grace's words when I'd rung her in a panic about how to handle this little liaison: "Take God into the room with you. Approach it with compassion and love. There's no point in causing any more pain for him or you."

We talk honestly and openly and, much later, I leave knowing that I too have played a significant part in this deceptive love affair. I can't yet forgive him, or myself, but I do feel more at peace.

Monday 26 July
Sydney

> "It is preoccupation with possession, more than anything, that prevents man from living freely and nobly." – *Bertrand Russell*

I'm stressed. I'm filled to capacity with consulting work and the writing of marketing plans. The end-of-year accounts need to be wrapped up and I've not even started culling and sorting out our belongings.

What shall I do next? Sort our personal and household belongings. Aided by the sweet warbling voice of Natalie Merchant, American folk-singer and writer, I devise a simple plan to treat this as a symbolic ritual rather than a chore. It's an opportunity to cleanse and detach from possessions that won't serve us in our new life.

With some trepidation I approach my wardrobe and drawers. Within an hour my bed is littered with the clothes, shoes, handbags and jewellery I no longer want. After I bag them all up I'm left with about a quarter of my personal possessions. Now there's no stopping me – I'm a woman on a serious mission.

By the end of the day I've all but finished the stocktake of our home and finalised the list of big items to be sold and given away. I estimate more than half our worldly belongings are about to find a new home. It's a cathartic experience. I'm detached from our possessions. They've served us well, but we no longer need most of them.

Billy arrives home and is astounded at the progress I've made. There are boxes everywhere and the kitchen is inaccessible so we enjoy takeaway noodles for dinner while I help him with his homework.

Tuesday 10 August
Sydney

"Feel the fear and do it anyway." – *Susan Jeffers*

I give Billy a big hug as I drop him at the bus stop. He's just been coasting through school in his last week. He's pretty excited about the move to Melbourne. What he's not so excited about is France – the fear of the big unknown.

We don't have any friends or family there and neither of us can speak more than a few words of French so it could end up being one hell of a long, lonely trip, or the most wonderful experience of a lifetime.

At home I look at my to-do list. Incredibly, it's shrunk from two pages to two lines. Now all we have to do is wait for the removalists.

I can't believe how calm and relaxed I am. I spend the rest of the day writing a last-minute marketing report until Billy arrives home from school.

The end of a huge chapter of our lives is just days away and we're both starting to feel incredibly sad, mostly about leaving our dearest Dash.

⚜ ⚜ ⚜

Wednesday 11 August
Sydney

> "Until this moment, I never knew how hard it was to lose something you never had." – *Unknown*

It's a very, very sad day. It's the day we hand over Dash to Maureen and her husband Mick. While Billy is at school I'm trying to distract myself from thinking about it by finishing off the marketing report.

Dash knows something is up. How could he not? There are boxes everywhere and people coming and going, and

Getting Unstuck

every now and then I'm tearing up and giving him spontaneous hugs.

I think back to the beautiful spring day we drove out of Sydney to the breeder's kennels. My friend Alison and Billy's friend Courtney came too. The kids were only eight, so sweet and innocent and excited at the prospect of a new pup.

The car had hardly stopped before the kids had opened their doors and raced over to the puppy playpen. The breeder opened the pen and one little guy, smaller than the rest and with a flat black coat, not curly like his siblings, ambled over to Billy, who was sitting on the grass. He promptly sat on Billy's lap, turned over and gazed up at him as if to say, "I'm yours." And that was it. By the time we'd arrived home, we'd named him Dash.

Now, after almost four years, we're about to give him away. Our only comfort is that the life Mick and Maureen will give him will be better than the one we can offer. They adore Dash and he adores them. I've no words to express my gratitude.

Billy arrives home from school and we head off to Mick and Maureen's for a quick walk and a beautiful roast dinner. When it's time to leave, Billy gives Dash a long, sad, tearful hug.

Our eyes are filled with tears while Dash's eyes are filled with confusion. We leave quickly and our hearts break at the sound of his whimpering.

"He'll be really happy here," I tell Billy. "We'll come and see him again on Friday before we leave."

Thursday 12 August
Sydney

"We must travel in the direction of our fear."
– John Berryman

Billy arrives home from his last day at school. He's just said goodbye to all his school friends and now he's about to say goodbye to his home, which is filled with boxes and bubble-wrapped furniture. He's sad and subdued.

Our friends turn up to take the last of the unwanted furniture and to toast our future. We're sitting around the dining table, listening to my French music collection, sipping Champagne and reminiscing about all the good times we've had in this home over the years.

James is here too, subdued and pensive, not imbibing like the rest of us.

I'm pensive, too. There are a million things I still want to say to him. I wish we could have one last evening together, to end our love affair as dramatically as it had started. But that's not possible. It's over.

When our friends leave, Billy and I spend some cosy mother-and-son time chatting. We settle down to sleep on mattresses on the floor, in what was once our lounge room, looking out over the lights of Coogee.

Getting Unstuck

Friday 13 August
Sydney

> "True love doesn't have a happy ending, because true love never ends. Letting go is one way of saying I love you." – *Unknown*

Friday the thirteenth. Lucky for some, and for us, I hope. It's 2pm and nearly time to hand over the keys. The removalists have taken our belongings to Melbourne and the cleaners have been. The house is now totally empty. It has a sad, hollow echo to it.

Billy and I go through each room, recalling experiences we've had there. We start in the front room, my office, where I would beaver away on my computer and occasionally look up at the trees outside my window to dream up new business ideas, new book titles and travel plans. I was often happy in my office.

In my bedroom I remember the first night we slept here. Billy was just 3½ years old. It was the official day of the end of my marriage. One night we'd been in our family home and the next night we were here. We had no furniture yet, just a mattress on the floor in this room. I remember laying here cuddled up to my son, waiting until he was asleep before breaking into silent tears. I can only imagine how lonely and sad his father must've been.

Still in that bedroom, I smile deviously to myself, recalling some of the more 'active' evenings I'd spent here when Billy was at his dad's. I never had a man sleep over while Billy was here with me, although Dash could probably tell a story or two.

We move on to the dining room. The dining table had been at the heart of so many wonderful Christmas celebrations, birthday parties and dinners.

I remember my crazy fortieth birthday party with 50 friends and the police paying us a visit around 4am. Then there was the curry evening I hosted after my trek in India. And there were many of Billy's birthday parties of course – like his fifth when my mum dressed up as a witch, despite it being a pirate party (so cool that my family does stupid stuff like that). And the year my dad tried his darnedest to disguise himself as Father Christmas only to be instantly recognised as Grand-dad. All of these special occasions come flooding back.

We pass through the kitchen – admittedly not my favourite room in the house. Is it a sin not to like cooking? I've just never really been creative in that area. I recall a few of the burnt offerings I'd served up over the years in this kitchen and move on to Billy's room.

In our time here, this room had been transformed from an aquarium to a Harry Potter theme, to a *Toy Story* theme and then finally a more grown-up youthful look masterminded by my clever interior decorator friend Jane.

In this room I'd lain next to Billy on his bed and read him nursery rhymes, fairy tales and Roald Dahl books, and told him some pretty pathetic made-up stories too. I'd watched him grow from a toddler to a kid and now a blossoming teenager.

Getting Unstuck

We enter the living room. Many times we'd snuggled up on the couch in this room to watch movies and our favourite comedies, like *Kath and Kim*. I even remember one Easter many years ago when Billy was with his dad, my friend Julie and I had watched 30 back-to-back episodes of *Sex and the City* in this room. We were both going through 'man pain' at the time, so it seemed like the only thing to do.

We head out to the balcony overlooking Coogee and lean on the rail to take one last look at the fabulous view and what has been our local community for many years. I have very mixed feelings about this balcony. In the mornings it was a place of happiness and serenity, a place for Sunday breakfast and basking in the sun and sitting with Dash. At night, sometimes, on my own, it was a place to retreat to glare at the stars and drink wine to numb my loneliness and feelings of abandonment, particularly around James.

We walk downstairs to the room beneath the house that had been the sleeping quarters for my sister Di for three years, and Julie for a year. It was then my office where Angela, Jennifer, Justine, Emma and Doris had come to work with me over the years. And it had then become home for Louise, then Stephanie.

That room had certainly been versatile – a home for some, and a place for me to grow my business too.

We stroll into the back yard that overlooks the ocean. Here is where we'd read books in the hammock, watch whales migrating along the coast and enjoy barbecues and back-yard games.

As a kid, Billy had stood at the steering wheel nailed to the deck on his cubby house dressed as *Toy Story's* Woody or Harry

Potter. It had been home to the vicious rabbit Poppy, which had bitten Billy one too many times and had to be given away.

And, of course, it was where we'd played with Dash and where he'd bask in the sun until the cat from next door taunted him enough to raise a bark from him.

There were so many happy memories in this house, and some sad. But it's now time to create a new home in a new town.

The agent arrives and I hand over the keys. Billy and I say goodbye to him, and the house, and leave in a hurry without looking back.

We pick up Dash for one last walk in our local Coogee community. He's overwhelmed to see us. Billy and I are just plain sad.

We take a walk along the main strip of Coogee and think about all the yummy meals and coffees and fun we've had in our favourite cafés and restaurants. We head towards the beach where every Sunday morning in summer since Billy was six we'd wander down, bleary-eyed, to Nippers.

It was where I'd overcome my fear of the ocean and become a Surf Life Saver, and had the immense pleasure of helping Billy and other young Nippers navigate the ocean and learn how to save a life too.

We walk along the beachfront towards the dog park and I recall all the runs and cliff-top walks I'd done over the years. We pass my old yoga studio overlooking the ocean, the playground where Billy had spent many hours swinging, climbing and playing make believe, and the rotunda in the park where each year we'd eat a picnic while watching a fabulous Shakespeare production.

Getting Unstuck

Then on we go past the jewel of Coogee, Wiley's Baths – the ocean-water swimming pool where we'd swim with the fish and marvel at the blue bottles, sea urchins, periwinkles and occasional octopus.

We continue walking south along the cliff-top around the dog park and down the boardwalk through the swamps where water trickles down into the Pacific Ocean. We end up at the rock pool we love so much and where Dash often took a dip.

We return north along the cliff-tops and back to the dog park. It's cold and grey and the ocean is putting on an uncommonly churlish performance. Maybe it knows we're deserting it.

That's when James arrives to say goodbye. We chat in a friendly, pleasant manner until Billy bids him farewell and jumps in our car with Dash.

Now it's just the two of us in this deserted, windy park, both bundled up in our coats, standing as close as we can get to each other. I've no idea what he's thinking. Is he sad? Is he relieved? Does he even care? I don't ask and he doesn't volunteer his thoughts either.

I offer up some feeble words. "Whatever has happened between us, I've played my part in it. I'll be okay and I know you will be too."

He doesn't really say anything in return. He just nods, smiles and looks so incredibly sad. The time for words is clearly over. We both know it's time to move on, for good.

We hug for what seems to be an eternity. I can physically feel the pain in my heart and I barely manage to hold myself together. It really does feel like it's the last time I'll ever see him.

Hastily I disentangle myself from his embrace, jump in the car and drive off.

We drop Dash back at his new home. We don't hang around. We simply can't. I know the sorrow and guilt will catch up with me later (and for Billy, too, I'm sure).

We spend our last night in Sydney at our wonderful friend Sheena's house with a group of our most special friends for one final farewell, a commiseration at our leaving and a celebration for our new adventures. It's a night of reflection and love and wistfulness for us all.

When at last I plop into bed exhausted, the grief of saying goodbye to our friends, to Dash, to James and to our beloved Coogee finally takes over.

Saturday 14 August
SYDNEY TO BEECHWORTH, VICTORIA

"Freedom lies in being bold." – *Robert Frost*

It's a gorgeous sunny Sydney day, perfect for the start of a long drive. The car is packed with our belongings for the 1037-kilometre journey along the Hume Highway to Melbourne. Billy and I are acting brave and try not to cry as we hug our friends goodbye and drive out through their gate.

It actually feels wonderful to be leaving and getting on with a new life. The decision to uproot our lives had been made just three months before. It had taken a lot of planning, action and fortitude to bring it all together and I'm honestly pretty exhausted by it all, yet satisfied and excited.

I'm closing a 10-year chapter of my life and am about to start a whole new one. I'm like a rose bush that's been pruned to the roots awaiting a rich organic fertiliser to grow again in a whole new direction. Everything in my life, and in Billy's of course, is awaiting renewal – our home, our lifestyle, Billy's school life, my career and, finally, my love life.

It's symbolic then, to be driving out of Sydney rather than flying. Somehow, getting behind the wheel of a car and driving with the bitumen beneath us and the open sky above, makes it seem more final.

Sunday 15 August
Beechworth to Melbourne

> "The journey of a thousand miles begins with one step." – *Lao Tzu*

We're continuing our journey to Melbourne after an overnight stay in historic Beechworth, famous for Ned Kelly, Beechworth honey and the Beechworth Bakery. It's getting colder and damper the closer we get.

As we enter Melbourne, the heavens in all their wisdom open up and welcome us with a torrential downpour of rain. The skies seem to be saying, 'Don't say we didn't warn you. Melbourne is a great city, but this is the reality of winter here. Like it or lump it!'

But not even the rain can dampen our spirits. By now we're pretty resilient and have greater things to focus on. I drop Billy at his father's house for his final week in Australia before we head off on our French adventure.

I spend a lively, chatty evening with my friend Anne and her daughter Amelia, who just five years ago also migrated south from Sydney. I'm comforted by the fact that at least I have one girlfriend in Melbourne to help make the transition easier.

Getting Unstuck

Monday 16 August
MELBOURNE

"Home is any four walls that enclose the right person." –
Helen Rowland

It's 9am and I'm waiting inside our new home for the removalists to arrive. The townhouse belongs to my ex-husband's wife and she's generously offered it to us until I buy a new home.

The removalists arrive and Billy and his dad turn up to help. By 5pm the house is completely unpacked and set up. Even the beds are made. Billy's step-mum turns up with a celebratory bottle of Champagne. A few hours later we're all mellow and exhausted and ready for bed.

Billy leaves with his dad for his other home. As I close the door behind them, I think how weird life is. Here I am, living in my ex-husband's new wife's townhouse and my ex-husband has just spent a whole day helping me unpack. Somewhere, somehow, I must've done something right over the years to be experiencing this generosity.

I think back on the many times I'd felt alone and lonely in Sydney when Billy went to spend weekends with his dad. Tonight I feel tired but happy as I climb the stairs alone to bed. Alone, but not lonely, in our temporary new home.

Saturday 21 August
Melbourne

"Cultivation to the mind is as necessary as food to the body." – *Marcus Tullius Cicero*

I'm at Melbourne's famous Prahran markets. The voices of the vendors touting their wares and the heavenly smell of coffee, flowers and cheese fill the air. I can only imagine how delightful it will be to shop at the daily open-air markets that Aix is so famous for.

I wonder what I might throw together for my lunch each day in Aix. Maybe pitted black olives, baguettes dripping in olive oil and balsamic, rabbit terrine, some brie, cured meat, a boiled egg or two and a simple salad of rocket, parmesan and pear sprinkled with walnuts?

I've only been in Melbourne five days and every one has been a gastronomic delight. I've been able to catch up with my darling friend Vesna, visiting from Adelaide, Anne again, and some long-lost friends from high school, all over superb food and wine. It's a culturally creative and very groovy city. The people are friendly and amiable and it's blissfully simple to get around. I'm almost feeling a little sad at the prospect of leaving so soon after arriving.

Getting Unstuck

Sunday 24 August
Melbourne

> "Where's the good in goodbye?" – *Unknown*

The atmosphere is a bit subdued today over our farewell yum-cha with Billy's dad and step-mum. I know both Billy and his dad must be feeling terribly sad at the prospect of not seeing each other for four whole months. I'm just thankful his dad has been so supportive of our adventure and can see the benefit in this experience for Billy.

We eat without chatting much, each of us preoccupied with our own thoughts and feelings.

On our way back to the townhouse I thank Billy's dad for his generous support and help in this big move.

"I really appreciate it," I tell my ex-husband.

I leave the three of them to say their own sad goodbyes.

Monday 23 August
Melbourne Airport

"A goal is a dream with a deadline." – Napoleon Hill

My dream is about to become a reality. Our suitcases are packed and the house has been put to sleep. We start our adventure in style in a luxury chauffeur-driven car that takes us right to the departure doors at the airport.

We're both excited and contemplative. I know there'll be as many trials as triumphs on this journey.

As the plane hurls itself off the tarmac into the grey Melbourne skies, I say to Billy with a smile, "Hang on for the ride. It might get rough at times."

And he knows I'm not just referring to the possibility of a turbulent flight.

2
Bonjour Paris!
Melbourne to Paris, France

Monday 23 August
Melbourne – Singapore – Paris!

> "Another word for creativity is courage."
> – *George Prince*

I love flying. Being held captive in one seat for an extended period, means I actually have to deal with myself. It's my sacred time to write in my journal, read, meditate and dream. I pull out *The Artist's Way*, the book that's been recommended to me as the perfect companion for my time in France. I open it to a random page and read.

"Develop interest in life as you see it; in people, things, literature, music – the world is so rich, simply throbbing with rich treasures, beautiful sounds and interesting people. Forget yourself." – *Henry Miller*

I'm aware I've been totally egocentric the past three months. It was all about me (and Billy, of course) and I simply didn't have the time or energy to focus on much else. I'd been steadily digging our way out of our old existence, shovel by shovel, until we'd made it onto this plane.

Now it's time to be inspired by a new country, a new culture, a new language, new food, new people and maybe even a new lover.

While I forget myself, maybe I'll discover a fresh new spiritual and creative self, who can write a brilliant book?

Bonjour Paris!

I have very few regrets in life, but there is one big one – that it's taken me so long to uncover and nurture my latent creativity.

As a child I was never really offered the opportunity to deeply explore my artistic or creative side. Parents and schools treated any creative or artistic pursuit as a mere hobby (and most still do) – something to be done in one's spare time and certainly not something that could be your future livelihood. So when I left school to become self-sufficient, I got a good job in a bank and settled into a comfortable corporate career because, after all, that's what pays the bills. Even when I started my own business nine years ago, I ignored the opportunity to be wildly creative.

Sure, I love my music, and going to the theatre and the cinema, and I read voraciously. But that's merely creative voyeurism. I think I've always been a frustrated artist – I just never knew what my artistic bent would be. In an attempt to discover it, I've tried piano lessons, singing lessons, dance lessons and acting lessons, but none struck a chord – until I started writing just five years ago.

I love the process of writing. I'm in pure flow when I write. I lose all track of time. I forget to eat and the household chores remain undone.

I can also write with my favourite music blaring in my ears. It fills my heart and inspires my thinking. The words flow from a place that's not of my brain but outside of me. They're channelled. That's not to say, the words are always brilliant. Often, they're not. But that's okay.

At the ripe old age of 41, I was able to produce my first book because I'd untapped this latent passion for writing. Better late than never, I suppose.

I have big plans to write another book while we're in France and I can hardly contain my excitement at the prospect of uninterrupted time to create my own personal masterpiece in a country that embodies creativity itself.

I'm itching to dive headlong into *The Artist's Way*, but close it quickly and shove it back into my bag. I want to start it once we're settled in Aix and Billy has started school, when I have the space and time to do it, and myself, justice.

I pull out *A Year in Provence* by Peter Mayle instead. Maybe I can learn a thing or two about writing from the master himself?

⚜ ⚜ ⚜

Tuesday 24 August
PARIS

"An artist has no home in Europe except in Paris."
– *Friedrich Nietzsche*

It's 7am. We've been in the air or in airports for over 30 hours. But it hardly matters that we've barely slept and are exhausted – we're in Paris!

Bonjour Paris!

As we wait patiently for our luggage, I observe our fellow passengers. I love people watching and airports are absolutely the best place for it. It's thrilling to listen to the lively accents of travellers from all corners of the world. I wonder where they've come from, where they're going and why. Work? A funeral? A wedding? A holiday? I wonder if they're living the life they'd imagined? Lastly, I wonder how many are on an extended sojourn like us? Not too many, I guess. Feelings of smugness arise. I beat them off and replace them with gratitude.

Finally the luggage arrives and we struggle out to a taxi.

"Bonjour. Je voudrais aller à Rue des Petits Carreaux, 2nd arrondisement, si'l vous plait," I attempt in my best French.

The driver shakes his head and responds in rapid indecipherable native tongue. It's impossible to respond so I pull out the map and pinpoint our destination. Bienvenue en France!

The taxi ride from the airport to the city centre is usually a disappointing experience in any city and our entry into Paris is no different. The highway is littered with fast-driving cars and lined with large, windowless apartment blocks and factories that seem to multiply before our eyes.

"Where's the Eiffel Tower?" asks Billy. "This isn't what I imagined Paris to be like."

I smile. "Close your eyes and have a nap and soon you'll see the real Paris."

Secretly, I'm disappointed too. My last point of entry into this great city six years earlier will remain forever etched in my memory. My girlfriend Cathryn and I had taken the TGV from London to Paris and the metro train to St-Germain-des-Près. As we emerged from the underground for our first foray into the streets of Paris we were greeted by snowflakes, the yummy smell of crepes and the twinkling of Christmas lights. There were bicycles weaving, bells ringing, motorbikes buzzing and Parisians jay-walking home with baguettes underarm and mobile phones on their ears.

The cafés were bursting with elegantly coiffured women with haughty dogs on their laps and nonchalant men with cigarettes held mid-air over intense, heart-felt conversations – no doubt about love lost and lust found.

I'd had an overwhelming feeling of love for this city I'd just stepped into. It took my breath away.

I know I'll regain this love, once we get into the heart of Paris. I just hope Billy feels it too. I gaze fondly at him resting on my shoulder and pray this experience will be a positive one for him. For not only has Billy had to deal with our move and everything that's entailed, he's also had to deal with a particularly aggressive onslaught of the big P – puberty. His voice is deeper, his shoulders have widened, he's grown about six centimetres in six months, has a little moustache and a monosyllabic dialogue, thankfully mostly reserved for his mother.

So while I'm super keen for him to take a childlike, wide-eyed, inquisitive approach to his time in France, I know that's not likely. I'll need to give him the space to do what makes him happy, even if that means Skyping his friends rather than exploring the Louvre.

Maybe through this process I'll learn to be less controlling with him and maybe he'll get to appreciate the education in life being bestowed upon him. We'll have our moments, of that I can be certain. I just hope they're manageable and we don't kill each other in the process. Should a mother even say that?

Bonjour Paris!

Finally we arrive utterly exhausted at the front of our apartment block on the most truly quintessential and exquisite Parisian street, Rue des Petits Carreaux. Like all apartments built in bygone eras there are no lifts, just four flights of narrow stairs waiting for us to heave and haul and puff our way up with our heavy suitcases. We both hope the trek will be worth it.

When we finally get there, we're not disappointed. The apartment is small and the kitchen is the size of a handkerchief but it's nicely decorated and perfectly clean. Most importantly – even more important than a comfortable bed or hot running water – is the fast, uninterrupted internet access! (Sad, I know, but the internet is our lifeline to family and friends.) So in all we're very happy with our new digs for the next eight days until we travel to Aix.

It's only lunchtime and we've hardly slept for two days. After unpacking and trying desperately not to collapse into our beds, we go back downstairs to explore our new local strip.

There are young, handsome men sitting in cafés drinking espresso and eyeing off the gorgeous young student-like women on bicycles weaving their way along the narrow cobbled street.

There are slick waiters taking quick cigarette breaks before resuming their impeccable, unsmiling table service.

There are elegantly dressed wafer-thin mothers walking their dogs with little kids in their oh-so-French outfits and matching berets.

The street is lined with exquisite-smelling fromageries, patisseries and boulangeries, cafés, restaurants and chocolateries. It's truly a sensory and rather opulent experience being in this street – until we come across the beggars.

I'm shocked by how many there are. It somehow gives the whole scene the dose of reality that perhaps it needs.

There's a migrant mother with a young girl and a well-trained dog laying perfectly still with sad, longing eyes and a small sign propped up in front of them: "J'ai faim". She's shaking a plastic cup for coins and beseeching us to make a small contribution, which I do.

And there's an irascible old man approaching unsuspecting customers in cafés as he does a shuffling two-step dance to a battered beat-box resting on his shoulder.

We pick a lovely café and take a seat facing the street, as one does when one is in Paris. It's the perfect place to watch people. Billy slurps his hot chocolate – chocolat chaud – and virtually inhales his croissant and remarks, "This is more like it."

⚜ ⚜ ⚜

Wednesday 25 August
PARIS

"The traveller sees what he sees, the tourist sees what he has come to see." – GK Chesterton

Bonjour Paris!

It's clear why they call Paris the City of Love. As we take our first metro train to the Eiffel Tower, a happy chap on an accordion serenades us with 'I Did It My Way' as we cross the bridge over the River Seine. The magnificent La Dame de Fer (Iron Lady) literally appears from nowhere. It's so incredibly, devastatingly romantic.

While I'm thrilled to be here with my son, I can't help but wonder how glorious it would be exploring this city with a lover. Not an old lover, like James, but a new one.

I can't believe it's just 12 days since our dramatic end. Of course it still hurts, and he still invades my thoughts more than I'd like, but I trust as each day passes he'll fade into the recesses of my mind.

They say the French would die for love. And maybe that's why I adore this place. As old as I am, as disenchanted as I've been and as betrayed as I've felt, I've always believed in love. I refuse to be a cynic about it. Without hope, faith and love, there's really no point.

But for now, I'm with my beautiful son who's awestruck at the sheer height and scale of the Eiffel Tower. His dad rings just as we're about to start our journey to the top of this incredible global icon. I can hear the excitement in his voice as he tells him where we are. It's a relief to see him so thrilled about being here.

We climb the steps to the first level and join an incredibly long queue waiting to go to the next level. It's bedlam and Billy wants out.

"Mum, I think we've come far enough – I can't be bothered going to the top. Let's go and get a crepe."

I'm about to respond with the travelling mother classic: "We've come all this way to Paris and you don't even want to go to the top of the Eiffel Tower!?!" But I stop myself.

"You know what, I'd rather get a crepe too."

So we descend and head straight to the crepe van to order a jambon et fromage (ham and cheese) crepe and sit on a bench overlooking the Seine. We gaze up at the Tower, instead of down from it with all the other tourists, and laugh at the touters running away from the police with their precious Eiffel Tower trinkets wrapped up tightly in white bed sheets.

It's seriously the best crepe on earth. One mouthful is all it takes for Billy to make his big announcement: "I love Paris."

Back at the apartment Billy has some computer time while I devour my *Lonely Planet* and listen to the music of Carla Bruni – singer, songwriter, ex-model and third wife of French president Nicolas Sarkozy.

Carla might be Italian-born but her music is distinctly of the French chanteuse variety, oozing with sexuality and love. There's really no better way to end the day in Paris – yes, PARIS!

Bonjour Paris!

Thursday 26 August
Paris

"It is compassion that brings you to Nirvana."
– *Buddha*

I can't move. My body feels like a block of cement. My eyes are open but they won't focus. Where am I?

It takes me a full five minutes to reach total consciousness and to realise I'm in another bed in another country, not in my old bed in Coogee.

I look at the clock. It's 10am. I've been asleep for 14 hours.

Jet lag had obviously hit with a vengeance. Billy is still sleeping like the teenager he's about to become. I take a quick shower, leave a note on his pillow and slip downstairs for a strong double espresso. I'm hoping it'll wake me up enough to write in my journal with some intelligence and clarity.

The topic for this morning's journal? My future work.

I'm not sure why I want to bring to life the debate about what's next with my career when we've just arrived in this gorgeous country. But my habit is usually to go with the first topic that jumps into my head. I've learnt to trust that what springs to heart and mind first must be transferred from pen to paper.

I write down this question: "If I could do anything in my

career, in this next great stage of my life, regardless of income, what would it be?"

I answer: "Write books." And then I write and write about all the other things I'd like to do – some big, some small, but all extremely meaningful to me.

After 30 minutes and three pages I close the journal and ruminate over my words with a second espresso.

Back to the apartment I trot to wake up a grumpy Billy from his 16-hour sleep for a trip to the Notre Dame.

As we make our way down the main street to the metro, we're distracted by a pungent aroma. We stop to investigate and discover a spice shop complete with hunting paraphernalia and moose heads watching over sack after sack of deep gold, orange and red spices, herbs and dried fruits from every corner of the orient. We stand there in awe breathing in the scent. The temptation to run our fingers through the spices and sample the dried fruits is stopped by a friendly Turkish man thrusting plastic bags towards us. We walk out with enough dried fruits to keep us regular for the next month and a sack of lovely rosewater and pistachio Turkish Delight.

We hop on the train and arrive at the main strip near the Notre Dame within minutes. Not for the first time, I pride myself on the choice of apartment location. A Croque Madame (a slice of bread topped with fat-laden ham, cheese and a fried egg) gets us both in the mood to play tourist for a few hours.

With not one crumb left on the plate we leave Café Touristique and present ourselves at the base of the stark and imposing facade of the Notre Dame Cathedral – Our Lady of Paris. It's an impressive monument to God, but I'm more interested in the view from the top than paying homage to a God I don't believe in.

I marvel at the glorious ability of man to conceive of, and then build, this magnificent cathedral, and I contemplate what the French peasants must have endured during its construction.

At the same time the indescribable wealth surrounding me is quite repugnant. The corporatisation of God (God Inc.) has always bothered me. Yet I know that Christianity, like most religions, has been hijacked and abused by man over the centuries and it really has nothing to do with God himself. He's the good guy.

I believe in a God, but she's grounded in Buddhist philosophy and holds a deep compassion for all people, of all religions, and I prefer to call her my Higher Power.

So for now, we're in this beautiful cathedral, this monument to God, with tourists crawling all over it and tour guides holding little flags in the air. We line up with all the others to climb to the top. And it's worth the wait. The Notre Dame is honestly the best place to get the most exquisite views of Paris, and the half-human and half-beast-like gargoyles are captivatingly intense.

On our way home we stop for an aperitif. We're enjoying the warm late-afternoon sun when a young lad appears at our table with a piece of paper in his hand. On the paper is a sentence or two, indecipherable to us. We shake our heads to indicate we don't understand and a waiter hurries out to wave him away. It's only then that I realise it was a decoy and that my phone has been stolen. I jump up to tell the café owners in my best animated Frenglish what's happened and lamely attempt to describe the kid, who I hadn't paid much attention to, while my brave son goes in search of him.

After no luck finding the boy or the phone, we leave the café to find a restaurant for dinner, all the while scanning the passers-by in the hope of spotting this kid.

"What would you do, if you did see him?" I ask Billy.

"I'm much bigger than him – I'd tackle him," Billy replies bravely.

Secretly I hope we never see this kid again. He can have my phone.

After dinner we stroll back past the scene of the crime to discover five policemen bearing down on a kid at the back of the café. His pockets have been turned inside out and he's looking scared and desperate.

We enter the café to speak to the police and examine the kid to see if he's the one who had stolen my phone. Although he's wearing the same standard black clothes we're both certain it's not him.

"Are you sure?" one of the policemen asks.

I wonder if he's hoping we'll say 'oui' so they can score a small victory for the evening. But he isn't the kid, we're sure, even though he probably belongs to the same gang. Reluctantly they let him go and the kid strolls off looking triumphant.

It's getting dark as we follow the police on a meandering journey through the back streets of Paris to the station to file a report. I just hope we can remember our way back home. Billy's now quite thrilled about the whole adventure as we're called up to see the head of police who thankfully speaks impeccable English. He questions us at length and the report is completed in no time.

"Au revoir. Merci."

On the way back to the apartment I curse myself for leaving my phone on the table so carelessly. Lesson learnt. At least it wasn't my wallet. That would have been far more problematic.

⚜ ⚜ ⚜

Friday 27 August
PARIS

"Home is not where you live, but where they understand you." – Christian Mortgensen

Getting from A to B in any new city requires a good map, comfortable walking shoes and at least some sense of direction (not one of my greatest assets). Getting from A to B with a 12-year-old who hates walking further than the distance from the couch to the fridge also requires great patience and superb bribing techniques.

The bribe? Food. We're on our way to find a restaurant that's been written up in *Lonely Planet* as a wonderful place to eat authentic, family-style French food. After about 30 minutes of walking I realise we're horribly lost.

I don't want to tell Billy because I know he won't be amused.

"How much further?"

"Just around the corner."

It's a line I've overused a bit in the past few days. He knows we're lost.

"That's it, I'm not going one step further. Let's eat here," he says, pointing to a café. We do and the experience is terribly unsatisfying and expensive, and we're both in antsy moods as we leave.

The truth is, the day was always going to be a bit of a disaster. We'd both woken up on the wrong side of our respective beds after the previous evening's events, and are feeling a little homesick (wherever home is).

We should've just gone back to sleep and woken up again – this time on the right side of the bed. But we didn't and I'd insisted on making the most of the day by going out to this restaurant that we couldn't find.

Now we have an afternoon to kill and attitudes in need of a thorough overhaul. I wonder what we can do to resurrect the day. A movie? After another hour of trudging around to find a cinema that screens movies in English, or at least with English subtitles, we find *Day and Night* – a movie I'd never even consider seeing in Australia.

Somehow, escaping for a couple of hours into a cinema and watching a movie in English, no matter how bad, takes away the feelings of isolation and homesickness.

Bonjour Paris!

Saturday 28 August
Paris

"Keep good company – that is, go to the Louvre."
– Paul Cezanne

Today, thankfully, I wake up on the right side of the bed with the promise of a lovely creative time ahead exploring the Musée de Louvre. While Billy's still sleeping, I slip downstairs to my new local for a café au lait and to read up on the tips for making our visit to this art museum – which is over 60,000 square metres and houses over 35,000 objects d'art – a pleasurable experience.

I'm buried deep in my *Lonely Planet* when a large tan dog comes up to my table and stares me straight in the eye. His look is at once sad and appealing, yet he's clean, looks well fed and is wearing a lovely leather collar. I scan the street for his owner but can't see anyone who fits the bill.

I'm tempted to pat him but decide to shoot him with my camera instead. I wish Billy were here to see this almost-human dog. That's when I realise he's begging, not for food, but money. He lowers his head and nudges a plastic cup towards me. As I reach for my purse, I hear a loud 'shoosh' behind me. It's the waiter chasing him away.

As grand as it is to (almost) climb the Eiffel Tower, survey Paris from the Notre Dame and explore the Louvre, little experiences like this are what make me love travel the most.

I rush back upstairs to the apartment in a jubilant mood to find that Billy has also got out of the right side of the bed. It's not too long before we're strolling down Rue du Louvre along the Seine. We stop to fuel up on citron et sucre (lemon and sugar) crepes before we attempt to tackle the most daunting art museum in the world.

We're about to enter one of the many glorious courtyards surrounding the Louvre when we hear the sound of metal hitting the pavement at our feet. I look down, worried, wondering if it's one of my earrings and spot what appears to be a man's gold wedding ring.

As I bend to pick it up a woman wearing a scarf and with pleading eyes, says, "Bonjour, it's your lucky day."

"It's not mine," I try to explain, "Is it yours?"

"No, it is for you, from God." She refuses to take it from me so I start to walk away with it.

"Please give money," she says, running after us. I shake my head apologetically as I press the ring back firmly into her hand.

So it's not even lunchtime and we've had a dog and a woman and numerous other street beggars attempt to relieve us of our money. I'm perplexed as to how to deal with the sheer number of them. Should I give them all money? Should I smile and shake my head? Should I talk to them? How do we show compassion in this city without going broke?

We join the queue at the Pyramide du Louvre. The entrance to the Louvre is one of the legacies of François Mitterand's presidency, and there's been much controversy surrounding the amazing huge glass and metal structure. I can understand why. It's futuristic design conflicts starkly with the classical architecture of the Louvre, but somehow it works.

Bonjour Paris!

We enter and head straight to sign-up for a guided tour of the highlights. I know if we venture off on our own, we'll end up losing each other and seeing lots but learning nothing. I'm taking the philosophy that less is more. If we see just 20 objects d'art and are inspired by their pure beauty and come to understand something of the life of the artist who created them, I'll leave 100 per cent satisfied.

Our guide arrives and off we go. We approach the Mona Lisa (La Joconde, which means happy, joyful woman), arguably the most famous painting in the world. We jostle with the throng of tourists to see this quite small, dark portrait housed behind bulletproof glass. I grab Billy and we anchor ourselves in a position that clearly indicates to our co-jostlers we're not moving, so we can appreciate her. Lisa is ample-busted, not that beautiful or fashionably dressed, yet her smile is enigmatic and engaging. She appears to have the secret to love and life dwelling in her heart and bosom. And she exudes a warmth that defies the darkness of the painting. She's ethereal in every way.

As we glide through the halls, listening attentively to our guide, I'm becoming increasingly interested in the art that depicts the female form.

I fall in love with the statue of Nike, the headless Winged Goddess of Victory (Samothrace). She's standing on the prow of a ship braced against the winds in a stance depicting strength, fortitude and triumph. Yet there's a softness and beauty about the way her garments swirl about her voluptuous body and the gentle curve of her wings. There's something masculine about her, but she's distinctly feminine. It's an awe-inspiring combination.

We move on to the gorgeous Aphrodite of Milo or the Venus de Milo, the Greek goddess of love and beauty, and the most famous Greek Hellenistic sculpture. I circle her three times, appreciating her from every angle. Even with a damaged nose and two missing arms, she's incredibly beautiful and serene. The muscles and flesh of her breasts and torso are unconstrained by her garments, which have fallen provocatively to her hips. There's an eroticism about her, a sense that her robes could fall to the ground at any moment exposing the full glory of her nakedness.

Is there any ending to the beauty housed in this most amazing art museum? I think not.

Billy and I happily make our way through the rest of the tour before trekking home for an aperitif. My journal is waiting patiently to receive my musings on the strength and beauty of the women I've gazed at today. Bliss.

Sunday 29 August
PARIS

"When women are depressed, they eat or go shopping. Men invade a country. It's a whole different way of thinking." – *Elayne Boosler*

Bonjour Paris!

I can't believe we've been here five days and I've not entered one shop in this exquisitely fashionable city. The truth is, I'm not a typical woman. While 'hate' is too strong a word for it, I strongly dislike shopping. The idea of a day in a completely soulless shopping centre gives me heart palpitations. If I have to shop, I need to see daylight between exiting and entering each shop so I can escape at the shake of a lamb's tail, if need be. And when it comes to clothes, I'm not a brand girl in any way, shape or form and would prefer to buy my clothes from Saint Vincent de Paul than Chanel. In fact, I'd say I'm pretty daggy when it comes to fashion.

However, I can't go to Paris and not go shopping. My girlfriends would never forgive me.

I know the only thing worse than shopping itself, is doing it with a 12-year-old boy in tow, so Billy's ecstatic when he's given a reprieve. I take a lovely long shower, make myself up, put on a dress and a few adornments and bid au revoir.

At my new local café I have a couple of strong espressos while making a shopping list. Okay. I'm ready. I gather my belongings and stride purposefully towards Les Halles. Funny, nothing seems open. Maybe I'm a bit early? Everything opens late here. That's when I realise it's Sunday and all shops are closed for the day.

The self-sabotage kicks in. I feel stupid and annoyed. Why didn't I know this? "Because vagueness is one of your specialities, Carolyn."

Every day numerous little frustrating situations seem to occur, like my phone being stolen or not being able to find a restaurant or losing a metro pass or being unable to communicate with the French on the most basic of requests. I think back to what I'm like in Australia. Yes I'm vague and a bit of a daydreamer there too, but it seems to be exacerbated here. I don't feel in control here. I feel like a misfit in this beautiful city.

'Who do I think I am, coming to this country not knowing anyone and unable to speak the language? Who do I think I am, disrupting my son like this and taking him away from everyone and everything that he loves?' On and on the barrage of self-abuse continues.

I walk back quickly to the park, plonk myself on the nearest bench, pull out my sunglasses and let tears take over. It's a full ten minutes or so before I have no tears left. It feels good to have had a cry, to grieve all that's been left behind and acknowledge my fear of the future. Who would have thought this torrent of self-abuse could have been sparked by a simple unsuccessful shopping trip?

I'd let fear take over. I know the only antidote to fear is love. One emanates from the mind, the other from the heart. I need something to turn my state from fear to love. Music. I grab my iPod and put in my earphones to listen to the sweet, sweet music of Angus & Julia Stone, my favourite brother-and-sister indie artists. I allow the music to permeate my mind and travel down to my heart. Ten minutes later, love reigns.

Bonjour Paris!

Monday 30 August
Paris

"For my part, I travel not to go anywhere, but to go. I travel for travel's sake. The great affair is to move; to feel the needs and hitches of our life more nearly; to come down off this feather-bed of civilization, and find the globe granite underfoot and strewn with cutting flints." – Robert Louis Stevenson

This week's been tough on Billy. The excitement and thrill of a new adventure have not overshadowed the pain and grief of leaving his dog, his dad and his home. Sadly, he doesn't have the maturity to know how to deal with it and of course crying is totally unmanly for a tough boy entering teenage-hood. Yet, I wish he would cry. I wish he'd sob his heart out, alone, or in my arms, and talk to me about it. I wish he understood that crying is a sign of strength, not weakness.

Instead of dealing with his pain, he's zoning out and retreating into his computer. Given a choice between seeing or doing absolutely anything he wants in Paris or a day on technology, the second wins hands down. It's becoming a sticking point and I don't know how to help him and get him inspired by everything that's waiting for us right outside our door.

I just have to be strong and ensure he has balance. It's not an option to let him spend all day on his computer. So today we're going on the open-top tour bus to marvel at the icons of Paris.

I recall my last time in Paris when, with just two days left before our departure, I was feeling guilty that I'd not even seen the Arc de Triomphe or strolled down Champs Elysees. So I'd decided a round on a tourist bus would fix that. I jumped on, went straight to the back downstairs and plugged in the earphones. Before the bus even took off I was snoring my head off. I awoke hours later at the same stop and hadn't seen a thing. Maybe taking a bus tour a mere three hours after getting home from a wild night at a jazz club wasn't that smart?

The experience is a little different today. We're sitting up top in Les Cars Rouge (the red bus) with the sun shining gently on our faces and not much chance of dozing off. Billy seems to be enjoying it – mostly because he doesn't have to walk anywhere or have me tell him, "It's just around the corner." As we turn on to the Champs Elysees, the Arc de Triomphe appears in all its glory. It's awe-inspiring. At last I get to see what I'd missed all those years ago. Nice.

Bonjour Paris!

Tuesday 31 August
Paris

"Some are kissing mothers and some are scolding mothers, but it is love just the same, and most mothers kiss and scold together." – *Pearl S Buck*

It's our last day in Paris so it's time to shop. I know 100 per cent the shops are open and where I'm going. Nothing's going to stop me this time. And it doesn't. Four hours is all it takes to buy a gorgeous pair of soft leather ballet flats, some gem-adorned sandals, a great metal-studded suede handbag, a cute embroidered shift dress with matching swing coat, postcards, a new journal, a few trinkets and a can of Coke.

Maybe I don't mind shopping that much after all. Exhausted, I trudge up the stairs to the apartment to show off my purchases to Billy. He's enthralled, particularly with the can of Coke.

With the can skulled before I even pour a glass of wine, Billy turns to me and says, "Mum, it's our last day in Paris, so I'd like to take you out to dinner to the Japanese restaurant tonight with the money Nana gave me."

For a complete minute I'm choked up and speechless. I feel an overwhelming love for this boy, my son – a love that completely wipes out the pain of the battles we've fought this week.

We've felt a little disconnected from each other as we've tried to deal with our own personal losses and the fears over the big changes in our lives. And now he's showing with one simple gesture that it will be all right, that he wants to connect with me, that he's accepted this journey we're on.

"That would be wonderful," I say, trying not to make a big deal of it.

We stroll down Rue des Petits Carreaux to dinner at the restaurant of Billy's choice. My Aussie son asks for a table at a Japanese restaurant in his best French. I smile at how gloriously multicultural the experience is.

Once happily seated, gazing at our Parisian friends strolling past just metres from our table, he orders dinner and drinks in French and we chat about stuff – not anything in particular and not anything deep and meaningful. We just talk. After we finish dinner, he asks for the bill 'l'addition s'il vous plaît' and he pays it with the 50 euros from his lovely Nana.

We wander home chatting about the things we've loved about Paris and what we're looking forward to about the next stage of our adventure. We are at one. I feel whole-hearted and content.

It's a lovely ending to our time in Paris and a fitting beginning for the new life we're about to embark on in Aix.

3
Our New Home

Aix en Provence!

Wednesday 1 September
Aix-en-Provence

"Why not make a daily pleasure out of a daily necessity."
– Peter Mayle

Today's the day we leave for Aix-en-Provence, our new home.

The next four months mean the world to me – a gift to myself to interrupt the old habits that no longer serve me, and an opportunity to form some new, and pleasurable daily habits. It's about creating the space to heal, to explore my creativity, to write, to enjoy all this gorgeous country has to offer, to make new friends and to set my intention for the future. I can't wait to get to Aix and get started!

We're safely on board the TGV with only a three-hour journey ahead of us. I open up my *Lonely Planet* and read up on it for what seems like the hundredth time: 'Aix-en-Provence is to Provence what the Left Bank is to Paris: a pocket of bohemian chic with an edgy student crowd. Aix is packed with bars, cafés, affordable restaurants and a wicked nightlife.' Sounds damn fine to me!

Aix has a population of 140,000 and is located in Bouches-du-Rhône, one of eight departments in the Provence-Alpes-Cote d'Azur region. The region is one of 22 mainland regions in France and borders Italy. It's about 650 kilometres

Our New Home

south of Paris and just 25 kilometres inland from Marseille, the second biggest city in France. There are over 30,000 students in this city who attend the few large universities and numerous language schools. Aix is famous for being the home of Paul Cèzanne, and its incredible food, flower, antique and collectible and jewellery markets.

I'm still comfortable I've made the right choice, despite not doing as much research as I would've liked. How can one be certain of anything anyhow? I know it'll be what we make of it.

We arrive at the Aix TGV station, me in a simple summer dress, Billy in a T-shirt and shorts. The sun is shining brilliantly and the sky is a deep blue that reminds me wistfully of home. The air is clear and the colours are somehow brighter and more vivid than in Paris. It's 28 degrees according to our friendly taxi driver, who happens to speak impeccable English.

I squeeze Billy's hand as we enter the city and circle the famous Rotunda fountain. Three noble women stand atop the fountain overlooking the city. Beneath them six chubby cupids sit atop six graceful swans spouting water from their beaks, while a pride of majestic lions takes guard.

We proceed down Cours Mirabeau, the main strip, where plane trees arch elegantly across the cobbled road to meet each other, their branches not quite touching. This strip is home to the most historical, elegant and gold-gilded restaurants in Aix, like Les Deux Garçons where Cézanne and Picasso would hang out for coffee and aperitifs.

The driver delivers us to 18 Rue Cardinale. We heave the bags out of the car, ring the buzzer for our landlady and haul the bags up the stairs to the apartment that's to be our home for the first four weeks of our trip.

We're greeted warmly by Laura, an attractive young French woman who shows us into the apartment. It's truly oh-so-French, with its solid old provincial furniture, big French windows, mirror above the marble mantle, a mix of abstract and portrait paintings and objects d'art, and a bookshelf full of the classics. There are two bedrooms – one with a writing desk for me – and a small kitchen, a bathroom with a bath and a large living/dining area. It's not posh or pretentious. It's rustic and full of character and it's perfect.

Laura pours us homemade lemonade and gives us instructions in a curious mix of French and English on how to use the various machines around the place. She's about to take her leave, when Billy pounces on her. "Don't forget the internet."

She gets Billy wired up and leaves us to it. We eagerly explore the apartment and bounce happily on our beds grinning at each other. If this is home, we're hooked!

Our New Home

Thursday 2 September

Aix

"You know, somebody actually complimented me on my driving today. They left a little note on my window that said 'Parking Fine'." – *Tommy Cooper*

Today we're visiting Billy's school, the International Bilingual School of Provence, which is over 10 kilometres away in a village called Luynes. If Billy's scared about the prospect of a new school, I'm absolutely petrified at the prospect of having to drive him there. In France, people drive on the opposite side of the road in cars with steering wheels on the other side of the dashboard and with manual gearshifts. I haven't driven a manual car since I was 16, when I first learnt to drive our family's FJ Holden.

Laura very kindly helps me negotiate the rental of a little baby blue three-door hatchback and shows me how to access the car park, a 10-minute walk from the apartment.

I take a deep breath as Billy fires up the Tom Tom. "Good start," I mumble as we kangaroo-hop out of the car park.

Just to reiterate, I'm petrified about driving in this country.

We enter the traffic. I'm driving with a concentration I've not had since I went for my license in that FJ Holden. Within five minutes I've had two gentle toots and no near collisions and within 15 minutes my heart palpitations and heavy breathing have slowed considerably.

"Mum, you're doing great," says Billy.

"Thanks, mate, I'm feeling okay now," I smile back.

After getting lost three times and resetting the Tom Tom more than once, we pull up in the gravel car park at the entrance of the IBS of Provence. The school is nestled amongst beautiful green rolling fields, creeks and ancient farmhouses. The main building of the school looks like what might've been an old farmhouse and is surrounded by tennis courts, a pool and a beautiful vine-covered courtyard.

We're greeted by the Head of Middle School, who's a lovely woman and makes us feel very welcome. Billy seems pretty happy about a few things. Firstly, that there'll be girls at the school. Secondly, that he doesn't have to wear a uniform. Thirdly, that he gets to do two hours of sport a day. On the other hand, he's not so happy at the prospect of 1½ hours of homework a day.

He leaves feeling a little less nervous – until he gets into the car with his mother again, that is. But we drive straight home and it's thankfully uneventful. A mid-afternoon wine – something I rarely indulge in – is a welcome relaxant after the stress of driving. I'm amazed that something so simple and seemingly insignificant, something usually so second nature, has given me such a sense of both fear and accomplishment.

Our New Home

Friday 3 September

Aix

> "When the student is ready, the teacher will appear." –
> *Buddhist Proverb*

The church bells of the nearby Saint-Jean-de-Malte gently bring me into a blissful state of consciousness. It's 9am and I've slept for over 10 hours. I lay here, listening to the bells, the chatter of people in the street below and the space between the sounds – the silence.

Now that we're here, settled happily and comfortably in our new home, my Higher Power has seen fit to bestow this sweet moment upon me, to gently coax me back into the spiritual practices I've been neglecting. I'm fully aware I've been running on adrenalin for the last four months and that I've forgotten how to stop the useless mind chatter and dwell in the present moment.

I think back to six years ago – another one of those defining moments in life. I'd asked Dad and his wife Edna if they'd take Billy and me on a tour to visit all the towns we'd lived in when I was growing up. As we pulled up at the front of our old homes and the schools I'd attended, we were reliving the happy (and some not so happy) occasions of my childhood. I was in the back seat on the long journey to our next town and Billy was fast asleep. I opened Eckhart Tolle's *The Power of Now*. He teaches that our mode of consciousness can be transformed and that the key to becoming free of the egoic mind and all its unhappy consequences is to become deeply conscious of the present moment – The Now. In that single moment, I was ready to be taught and my teacher appeared. The irony didn't escape me that I was discovering the power of 'now' on a trip dedicated to digging up my past.

And now in my bed in this beautiful apartment, all these years later, my Higher Power is reminding me to exist wholly in this present moment. She's giving me permission to stop running and doing and planning and thinking about the past and what might happen in the future and everything I've had to do to get us to France. She's giving me permission to just be here right now. What seems like an hour passes as I lay there observing my breath and the contents of my room and listening to the sounds outside my door.

I'm awakened from my blissful state by Billy's complaining that he's hot and hungry. So after we're both fed and watered, we head out to the nearest swimming pool to cool off. We dive in and swim a few laps before stretching out on our backs in the magnificent, welcoming sun of Provence. Divine.

Our New Home

Saturday 4 September
Aix

"One of the very nicest things about life is the way we must regularly stop what we are doing and devote our attention to eating." – Luciano Pavarotti

Food shopping in Sydney had always been a chore. Each weekend I'd prepare a list, drive to the shopping centre, fill a trolley with goods from the supermarket, stock up at the butcher, the gourmet deli and the fruit and vegetable store, drive home and unload it all. A week later I'd clean out the fridge and throw out half the perished produce I'd intended to cook but hadn't and start the process all over again. I'd unconsciously become stuck in a wasteful consumption cycle.

Today I start a whole new approach to shopping and eating. I'll walk to the markets every day and only buy what we'll eat that day. And there'll be zero wastage.

We follow our noses down Rue d' Italie towards Place des Precheurs (Preachers' Place). The sight of the farmers markets bursting with people and noise and smells, and the bountiful, beautiful, just-picked produce of regional Provence is heart-warming indeed.

I'm grinning stupidly as we make our way around the stalls buying the familiar fruit and vegetables, and then on to the less familiar – the many varieties of cheeses and olives, the spices and herbs, tapenades, olive oils, honeys, lavender products, many varieties of mushrooms, cured meats and salamis, nougats and sweets, baguettes and breads of every description. We carefully avoid the van selling cheval (horse) products – for now, anyway.

And the best part? Billy is relishing this shopping experience, too, as he taste tests his way around the stalls and helps make our buying decisions.

Our bag is filled with glorious fresh produce for petit déjeuner (breakfast) and déjeuner (lunch) and dîner (dinner). There's not one packaged item and for the first time in years I'm totally inspired to cook again.

After buying our produce from the friendly and patient stallholders we stop at the most exquisite patisserie to buy what will become Billy's absolute favourite – a mini citron meringue pie. We find a cosy café for une café and a chocolat chaud. Billy indulges in his pie and I indulge in a spot of people-watching. I can't believe how at home I feel. J'adore Aix en Provence!

Our New Home

Sunday 5 September
Aix

> "What lies behind us and what lies before us are tiny matters, compared to what lies within us."
> – *Ralph Waldo Emerson*

It's 8am and today I start to untap my latent creativity with the support of *The Artist's Way*. I'm feeling a bit daunted and a million questions come to mind. What if I get halfway through it and abandon it? What if it doesn't help me write my book? What if it brings up emotional stuff I can't deal with? What if my creative vein is completely blocked and unable to be tapped? What if, what if, what if…

So to avoid having to get started on my own creativity, we explore the cultural creativity of Aix instead. We walk along Cours Mirabeau and visit the Musée Granet to see the Alechinsky exhibition and get a sneak preview of the life of Paul Cézanne. We stop to listen to the soulful singing of an organ grinder and give him a few gold coins. Then we chance upon an authentic Provençale parade backed by drums and tin whistles. We lick our lemon and mango gelati while we wander around the streets marvelling at the statues, sculptures and fountains on every corner, and we pause outside the cathédrale to listen to the pure voices of the choir.

There's a feeling of joie de vivre, a general air of happiness and contentment that permeates Aix and awakens every one of my senses on this bright and sunny Sunday.

Now we're home. We pack Billy's bag for school, lay out his best shorts and T-shirt for the morning and eat a delicious platter of cheeses, olives, foie gras and crunchy baguettes dripping in olive oil from the local region.

Billy has a couple of hours to himself while I retreat to my room and tentatively open *The Artist's Way*.

> *Many of us wish we were more creative. Many of us sense we are more creative, but are unable to effectively tap that creativity. Our dreams elude us. Our lives feel somehow flat. Often we have great ideas, wonderful dreams, but are unable to actualise them for ourselves. Sometimes we have specific creative longings we would love to fulfil – learning to play the piano, painting, taking an acting class, or writing, or sometimes our goal is more diffuse. We hunger for what might be called creative living – an expanded sense of creativity in our business lives, in sharing with our children, our spouse or friends.*

After reading the story of the author Julia Cameron's creative and spiritual journey, and the basic principles of the program, I sign a contract to commit myself to this program.

I, Carolyn Tate, understand that I am undertaking an intensive, guided encounter with my own creativity. I commit myself to the 12-week duration of the course.

I, Carolyn Tate, commit to weekly reading, daily morning pages, a weekly artist date and the fulfilment of each week's tasks.

Our New Home

I, Carolyn Tate, further understand that this course will raise issues and emotions for me to deal with.

I, Carolyn Tate, commit myself to excellent self-care – adequate sleep, diet, exercise and pampering, for the duration of the course.

Signed Carolyn Tate, 5 September 2010.

There's no backing out now. While I've signed many contracts in the course of life and business, I've never signed a contract with myself. Somehow I feel this is going to be the most meaningful contract I've ever made. My body is vibrating with anticipation, for tomorrow I start my morning pages – three full freehand pages of writing to be done every single morning on waking, no judgement and no filtering.

⚜ ⚜ ⚜

Monday 6 September
Aix

"Education is what remains after one has forgotten everything he learned in school." – *Albert Einstein*

The alarm buzzes annoyingly just out of arm's reach. It's only 6am, the earliest I've woken in days and I'm grumpy.

I open my clean white journal and write:

These morning pages are a drag and it's only day one...

Brilliant start. I'm writing down any bit of rubbish that comes to mind. After 30 minutes I've produced three pages of pure mindless drivel. It's not the way I usually write so it's going to take some getting used to. I snap my journal shut and get up to run the bath for Billy.

I forget myself and concentrate on him. He'd been up most of the night worried and anxious about his first day at school. And now I'm as anxious as he is as he takes a bath, dresses in his self-selected uniform and tries to swallow breakfast. He's not saying much and neither am I.

We arrive at school (with no thanks to the Tom Tom again) and hide the little baby blue between a couple of enormous and expensive-looking four-wheel drives. With some trepidation we head into the school courtyard and stand bewildered within the gathering crowd of students and parents. The kids seem very cool and fashionable and I'm wondering why Billy had insisted on wearing his daggy surf shorts on the first day. He's looking at me scornfully, as if to say, 'Why am I wearing this? What are we doing here? Why are you doing this to me?'

We're waiting for Billy's grade, 4ème (Grade 8), to be called when we're told they're staggering the start times. His class doesn't start until 10.30am and we're two hours early.

"Didn't you read the email and timetable we sent out?" asks an incredulous teacher.

Obviously not.

We drive into Luynes and find a café where Billy fully deserves the two hot chocolates he consumes.

Our New Home

Take two. We're back at the school and Billy is being called up with the other kids to sit in the canteen where each day he'll get served a hot lunch. Oh, the joy of not having to pack daily lunches! For the rest of this year I won't have to clean out mashed up, half-eaten sandwiches or squishy apples from the bottom of his bag, or throw out a completely untouched lunch on the days he decides to play sport instead of eat.

He waves me goodbye with a faint smile and a look of fear as he enters the canteen. I feel sorry for him and just pray his first day will be okay.

I arrive home and twiddle my thumbs over a cup of coffee. It feels strange without Billy. What should I do today?

First, go to a doctor to get rid of the dry, annoying cough I've developed. It isn't really turning into a cold but seems to be getting worse, and I'm a bit worried about it – firstly because I never get sick and secondly because, if it becomes debilitating, I have no-one to look after Billy.

I know I'm being completely neurotic and irrational, which is very unlike me, but that is how I feel and the fact we are fully alone here really hits me.

So in an attempt to self-diagnose I do an online search for my symptoms, which turns up a few drastic possibilities like emphysema, whooping cough, bronchitis or pneumonia.

Then I realise the doctor I've been recommended to see speaks very little English, so I spend an hour writing down what I'm going to tell him and finding the French word for each of the illnesses I'm anxious to eliminate – emphysème, coqueluche, bronchite et pneumonie.

I arrive at the clinic to discover a very handsome doctor who speaks far better English than I'll ever speak French. After a thorough examination he laughingly eliminates all of my self-diagnosed illnesses and explains that it's an allergic reaction to the plane trees in Aix. I walk out giggling to myself and feeling a little idiotic but relieved with a script for allergy tablets.

"So, how was it?" I ask with a little trepidation, as Billy jumps in the car with a pretty blank look on his face.

"Okay," he says. "I can't understand a lot of what everyone says. They all speak French all the time. I got zero out of 10 for my French test. But we got to play two hours of sport and the other kids are fairly nice. I met some kids from England, Ireland, Mexico and Italy."

And in the same breath he turns his mind to his stomach.

"Did you get a baguette today? And did you get me a citron meringue pie from the boulangerie? And what are we having for dinner tonight?"

I laugh out loud and outline the evening's menu for him, which turns his blank look into a big grin.

Our New Home

Tuesday 7 September

Aix

"When you were born, you cried and everybody else was happy. The only question that matters is this: When you die, will you be happy when everybody else is crying?" –
Tony Campolo

There's simply no escaping routine. The alarm is ringing again and the morning pages beckon. I feel a lot of resistance to writing them.

This morning they start like this:

What are we doing here? What if it all fails and Billy hates school and can't cope with the language barrier?

And later:

I still think of James daily but without the same intensity and only briefly. No more noncommittal men…

I feel childish and self-obsessed as I write, but the contract keeps me writing. I've been warned the first two weeks are the toughest.

It's Billy's second day at school and my second day to myself. As I drop him off and wave goodbye and drive home, I reflect on our relationship. We've depended heavily on each other for the last 10 years but never more so since we've been in France. I decide this trip will be the stepping-stone to a more healthy interdependence as he enters the teenage years and we return to Melbourne.

Another critical element to creative recovery is that you must undertake one creative activity, alone, each week. So today is a freelance creative day just for me – my weekly artist's date with myself.

I take my camera on an excursion and shoot everything that captures my eye – the small stuff above and beyond the obvious tourist attractions. I photograph the windows in buildings, the hidden doors and laneways, and the small statues that go largely unnoticed. I approach my artist's date with a photographer's eye, not a tourist's eye. It's enthralling and illuminating and I love it.

It's 9.30pm. I can hear Billy restless in his bed attempting to get to sleep. He calls out, "Mum, I can't sleep."

"What's on your mind, mate?" I enter his room.

Tears well in his eyes and erupt into big, deep gulping sobs.

"I hate school. I miss Dad. I miss Dash. I miss my friends in Sydney. Why did you bring me here? I want to go home."

I lay down next to him, rubbing his back. I let him cry, not responding directly to his comments, but still showing empathy for his pain and acknowledging how hard it is for him. He cries for a long time. I have no idea how long. Then he falls into a deep, deep sleep. At last the dam has broken.

Our New Home

Wednesday 8 September
Aix

"One is wise to cultivate the tree that bears fruit in our soul." – Henry David Thoreau

I wake this morning and hurry through my morning pages. They're filled with questions of self-doubt.

Did I do the right thing bringing Billy here? Was I being selfish? What can I do to help him get through this? Shall I call his Dad?

As I wake Billy I'm fearful he'll refuse to go to school and demand to be sent home on the next plane. Thankfully when I do, he actually seems more at peace and doesn't even mention last night.

We go about our preparations for school like nothing had happened but he's very silent as I drop him at the school gates.

I'm really worried about Billy and need someone to talk to about it. I would normally call Grace for help, but with the time difference, it's impossible right now.

Just as I'm feeling helpless and alone, my friend Julie calls on Skype from the US. She just listens to my fears and worries, as I've done for her many times before. She doesn't judge, give unsolicited advice or make light of my fears. After an hour with her I feel much better and have some ideas on how to help Billy through this tough time.

School finishes at 1pm and we decide to see a movie – something that's familiar and Australian. *The Tree* is a beautiful movie – a rare union of both French and Australian filmmaking talents – about a family dealing with grief after the death of a husband and father. The family live in quintessential outback Australia near a huge Moreton Bay fig that's incidentally also the scene of the man's death.

The tree gains a life of its own and soon becomes integral to the healing of the family it shelters. I cry and Billy nudges me and smiles.

After the movie we indulge in gelati and chat about the movie. It's a nice way to end the day and makes us both feel a little less lonely and isolated from the country and family we both love.

⚜ ⚜ ⚜

Thursday 9 September
Aix

> "Happiness is when what you think, what you say and what you do are in harmony."
> – *Mahatma Ghandi*

Our New Home

The morning pages flow a bit easier this morning and Billy seems happier about going to school after announcing last night he's made some new friends.

After I drop him off, I put on my running gear and walking shoes and head out into the beautiful brilliant blue sunshiny day to take a walk (and tentative run) to my local park, Parc de la Torse.

I've decided to get back into my three most enjoyable modes of exercise while here – running, yoga and swimming. I haven't run for over three years, so I'm feeling a bit of trepidation about how I'll perform and if my knees will agree to support me again after all this time.

As I walk down the stairs into the park, I notice the leaves on the plane trees are already starting to fade into a gorgeous autumn gold as they dart about in the breeze with the sun's rays piercing through them to the freshly mown grass beneath.

As my fast walk turns into a trot, 'Glitter in the Air' by Pink comes through my headphones: 'Have you ever thrown a fistful of glitter in the air? Have you ever looked fear in the face and said I just don't care?' In that single exquisite moment I feel a surge of pure joy and freedom. I simply can't believe I'm here in this beautiful country, in this beautiful park on the other side of the world!

Billy comes home much happier, chatting about his new friends at school and telling me which teachers he likes and doesn't like, and how he's finding the school work compared to Sydney, all while munching on a crunchy baguette.

For dinner I serve up Provèncale Chicken washed down with Pamplemouse (grapefruit) lemonade. I'm not quite a Julia Childs yet, but Billy relishes every last mouthful. All that matters for me in that single moment is that my son is happy.

Friday 10 September
Aix

"Creativity takes courage." – Henry Matisse

I've been here a full nine days and not written one word of my book.

Despite doing my morning pages every day and my homework religiously, I've conveniently not found the time to start writing it.

I keep allowing myself to be distracted by all the temptations outside (and inside) my door in Aix – the markets, the shops, the cafés, the art, exercise, cooking, homework and Skyping friends. Even cleaning the apartment and doing the washing is preferable to facing my fears and writing the opening sentences of my book. I'm blocked and I lack courage.

In my desperation to find inspiration, I create my own affirmation: *I, Carolyn Tate, am a brilliant and prolific writer and author. My creativity heals my readers and myself, and leads me to truth and love. I live and work globally while earning an excellent income from my writing.*

I take some bright yellow cards, pens and stickers, bought at the most excellent papeterie (stationery store) on my artist's date, and write the affirmation again in my most abundant and flowing handwriting. I place a big red velvet love heart under it and surround it with sparkly stars. I feel a bit silly and childish and have a fair degree of scepticism.

I can't get my head around it, so I walk out the door to Thermes Sextius, the famous thermal springs and spa, for a few hours. Maybe some extended time in the steam room will unblock my creative pores and cleanse me of my self-doubt?

Saturday 11 September
Aix to Arles

"Adventure must start with running away from home." –
William Bolitho

Have car. Must explore.

I've hired the car for just one month so I want to make the most of it and explore the countryside. I've made a deal with Billy for the next three weeks that one day of each weekend will be spent exploring and the other day can be spent resting and doing what he wants.

So today we're driving to Arles in the Camargue, about 60 kilometres northwest of Aix.

We arrive in the midst of market time. The roads are blocked and there's not a park in site. After doing a few laps of the town we find a park and go to explore the endless markets. We stop to take a photo of a pig's head on a platter, eyes intact and tongue protruding, and we sample and buy the best ever mango nougat and wild boar salami.

The remarkable Roman amphitheatre, Les Arenes – the venue for chariot races and gladiatorial conquests that took place around 50BC – is now the venue for the famous ferias (bull-fighting festivals) and dominates the landscape of this incredible town. The enormous crowd, which seems to be swelling by the minute, is here for the last day of the Feria du Riz where the Matador will fight the kings of the Camargue, the bulls.

We get chatting to an American tourist who excitedly explains that he'd participated in the running of the bulls this morning, which explains the reason for all the huge metal rails in the centre of town.

We follow our ears to stumble upon a rowdy, festive brass band – a gang of 20 guys and girls all dressed in outrageous and scanty hot pink outfits of their own design, as they play an adulterated version of 'When the Saints Come Marching In'.

There's no conductor, no order and no quest for perfection in their performance. They just play in a big huddle with the crowd dancing around them and egging them on. The pure joy emanating from the band and its adoring fans could have healed the world.

And more wonders of Arles spring forth.

Vincent van Gogh is the hero of Arles. The Dutch painter moved here in 1888 from Paris to paint with a fervour inspired by the intense light and bright colours of the Camargue. Allegedly, an argument between Gaugin and van Gogh fuelled by absinthe was the catalyst for van Gogh to lop off his ear and led to his voluntary entry to a mental asylum in nearby St Remy de Provence, where he painted another 150 canvases. At the age of just 37 he shot himself, having sold just one of his paintings. It was another 10 years before his art would receive recognition around the world. Why do so many artists suffer for their art?

Then, as if we haven't had enough senses stimulated today, we witness the young men of Arles, bullfighters in training, in a bull-taunting contest. There are about eight boys, just a little older than Billy, in a large ring. Young bulls, one at a time, are prodded and shoved out of the back of a truck into the ring. The boys take it in turns to run from one side of the ring to the other, with the objective of tipping the bull on the forehead as it charges towards them. Billy is grinning from ear to ear, astounded at their bravery.

"This is pretty cool," he says. I'm not sure if it is cool or cruel, but I don't say anything.

It's now evening and we're back in Aix at Cathédrale Saint Sauveur, about to watch the Festival Berlin Orchestra play Vivaldi. It's not typically the kind of performance I'd go to, but I'm keen to expose us both to the arts in whatever shape or form is available here.

As we sit up the back on a hard pew in the cold church, Billy grumbles "What are we doing here? This is going to be boring!"

"It will be, if you let it be," I tell him, with a philosophical quip, which he fully understands but chooses to ignore.

The orchestra starts and the sound reverberates around the church. While it's truly beautiful, neither of us is getting hooked on the classics, that is until the beautiful female tenor starts to sing 'Ave Maria' with the most pure, chilling voice I've ever heard.

Billy sits bolt upright in the pew and watches and listens, totally mesmerised until the last note. Then he claps until his hands hurt.

Sunday 12 September
Aix

"I hold this to be the highest task for a bond between two people: that each protects the solitude of the other." – Raina Maria Rilke

Today is a quiet day, a day of solitude. We're settled and at peace in our own space. While Billy does his own thing, I read a lot and write not a word.

Our New Home

Monday 13 September
Aix

"Your friends will know you better in the first minute they meet you than your acquaintances will know you in a thousand years." – Richard Bach

This morning I'm journalling about the negative self-talk that's keeping me blocked creatively.

This book is just a pipe dream. I don't even know what I'm going to write about. There's no way I can make a career or living out of writing...

Then, gradually, my comments get more positive.

I've written two books before. When I set my mind to something, I make it happen. Coming to France is an example of that. I'm a great writer and even if I'm not, writing makes me happy. I'm going to start writing this afternoon after French school. The end.

Then I rewrite my affirmation three times, before getting Billy up for school and getting ready for school myself.

I walk Billy to the bus stop and head off to school to start the two-week language course I've enrolled in. When I arrive, there must be at least 50 people lined up for various courses.

We're tested so we can be put into the right class level. My result is as good as Billy's on his first day at school, so I'm put into Française Gènèral Plus (FG+), the absolute beginners class. I smile at myself. I'm not fussed. If I make some new friends and master just some of the basics so I don't feel like a complete outsider, then I'll be happy.

The morning is fun and I meet all sorts of interesting people, but by midday my mind is preoccupied and I'm itching to get away so I can start writing.

On the way home I pick up a baguette and take a little wander around the streets close to home – anything to avoid actually writing those first words. And that's when I discover Book in Bar, an exquisite English bookshop that reminds me of my favourite bookshop in Bondi, Gertrude and Alice.

I hesitate for a very long time at the door. Should I go in or not? If I do, I might not come out. If I don't, then I've no option but to go home and write. After a full minute of indecision I decide to enter the bookshop anyway. My worst fears are realised when I emerge over three hours later. It's just too late to write anything now, particularly as I have Susie, my neighbour from upstairs, coming for dinner.

I'd met Susie from California just two days before. I was trudging up the stairs to our apartment, weighed down by a bag of delectable fresh produce from the markets, when she appeared on the stairs before me. We smiled at each other and introduced ourselves. I noticed the mischievous twinkle in her eye and liked her immediately. Within no time we were plonked down on the couch drinking coffee, laughing and sharing stories. We became instant friends and by the time she'd left, she'd accepted my invitation to dinner.

We savour a basic meal of cheeses, olives, baguettes and pasta accompanied by a pinot gris and lots of laughs and stories. I

Our New Home

can tell Billy likes Susie because he converses with her animatedly throughout the meal and then is eager to impress her by clearing up the table, without a word from me.

"That was very impressive," I say as he goes to bed.

"Thanks Mum, but don't get used to it."

So with dinner under my belt, but still not one word written, I retire to bed to beat myself up about it. I wonder why I can't get started. I came here ready to write *Real Women* but now I'm here I don't seem able to muster up the ability to write about other women's journeys, particularly as my own is unfolding right before my eyes. So as I turn off my bedside light to go to sleep, I ask myself, "Should I be writing *Real Women* or should I be writing a book about our own journey?"

Tuesday 14 September
Aix

"I dream my painting, and I paint my dream."
– *Vincent Van Gogh*

The morning pages answer.

Write about your own journey and this time in France.

Capture this experience while you're having it. It's essential for your healing and eventually it will help other women too.

I'm so happy as I finish my morning pages. It just feels right. I take a quick jog and get us both organised for school.

I don't want to go to school, but of course I do. When it's over I virtually run home, wolf down a salad, grab my computer and head to Book in Bar where I choose a secluded corner table with a comfortable chair.

A million questions fling themselves at me. Shall I write it as a dairy or in chapters? What period of my life shall I write about? How honest and vulnerable am I prepared to be? How much do I include about Billy? What if it brings up stuff that's too painful? Will I have the guts to publish it? Will anyone even want to read it? And the questions keep coming.

I wander around the bookshop, tears threatening to erupt. I choose a book from a shelf, open it to a random page and read for as long as it takes to regain my self-composure.

I return to my chair and take a deep breath to consider all the options. I make a snap decision. I'll write it as a diary from the day I decided to disrupt our lives (17 May 2010) to the day I leave Aix (1 January 2011). I check the calendar on my computer and check the period of time I'll be writing about – 238 days – and then the number of days I have to write it – exactly 108.

I open a blank white Word document and entitle it *My Book*.

Then I close my eyes and cast my mind back to that fateful day in Coogee, Sydney where I'd decided to irrevocably disrupt my life, and Billy's. I tentatively write the opening lines. A volcano of words finally erupts from my belly onto the page. There's no going back.

Our New Home

Four hours later I look up to discover I'm the only person in the place. Reluctantly I leave to meet Billy at the bus station and walk home with him. I don't mention my book. It's a secret for now.

Wednesday 15 September
Aix

"Music does bring people together. It allows us to experience the same emotions. People everywhere are the same in heart and spirit. No matter what language we speak, what color we are, the form of our politics or the expression of our love and our faith, music proves: We are the same." – John Denver

Day eight of school for Billy and day three of school for me. I'm loving the French language but am deeply perplexed by its complexity. Mastering the French verb is an almost impossible task – j'aime (I love), tu'aimes (you love, informal), vous aimez (you love, informal), nous amons (we love), ils aiment (they love).

Not to mention le numbre. Ninety is actually soixante-vingt-dix (sixty, twenty, ten). I wonder why they don't have a number for ninety, like they do sixty (soixante) or why it isn't just trente-trente-trente (thirty, thirty, thirty). That would be much easier for us not-so-bright Anglais speakers. While I'm getting the hang of some of the basics, I'm not sure I have the mental capacity to write a book and learn a new language at the same time.

I leave school to pick up Billy from the bus stop as he finishes at 1pm today. We walk home quickly so he can Skype his dad before playing on the computer. I'm frustrated. I want to write, but we only have one computer and I'm not prepared to fight over it. So I don't write and do extra French homework instead. Mental note to self: get Billy his own computer ASAP!

It's now evening and we're driving in our little blue car to Venelles, a village about 15 minutes out of Aix, for dinner with Agnés and Richie and their twins Jade and Inés. Ever the opportunist, I'd asked our French Sydney neighbour Xavier if he knew anyone in Aix. It turned out he had a second cousin living here, so he'd kindly introduced us by email.

Their hospitality is outstanding and within no time we're made to feel right at home as we eat our way through the national dishes of France and talk about the idiosyncrasies of Australians and the French and music.

Richie announces his favourite band ever is Australia's Midnight Oil and his favourite song is 'Beds are Burning'. I'm thrilled and tell him everything I know about the most incredible band that I love and grew up with.

Billy proudly tells Richie that he once shook Peter Garrett's hand (sadly as a politician, not the lead singer of the best ever Australian rock band). While the French are brilliant in

Our New Home

99 ways, the one thing they're definitely not brilliant at is rock and pop music, so most French are huge fans of Australian, English and American bands.

As we bid farewell and hop in the car, praying that the Tom Tom will get us home, Billy says, "You know, Mum, music really is the language of the world." How did my son get to be so philosophical at such a young age?

Thursday 16 September
Aix

"We must do away with the absolutely
specious notion that everybody has to earn
a living. We keep inventing jobs because of this
false idea that everybody has to be employed
at some kind of drudgery. The true business of
people should be to go back to school and
think about whatever it was they were thinking
about before somebody came along and told them
they had to earn a living."
– *Buckminster Fuller*

I'm tired this morning as I write.

Are these pages really achieving anything? I feel like I'm just writing in circles. Can't I just write something profound for once?

And then James comes bursting into my mind and I can't help but write down all the things I hate about him and myself for wasting my time on him.

My vitriolic rants fill a full page. When it's over, I feel much better and I end my pages with, *I'm okay. Be patient.*

After French school I have lunch with Lucia, my new Italian friend from French school. She tells me her story. At the age of six she'd wanted to be an artist and she'd been told she really had talent. As she got older she was encouraged to ignore her creative dreams, to study hard, go to university and pursue a corporate career, because that's the best and most socially acceptable way to earn a living. Now at age 34, she's not picked up a pencil or a paintbrush for over 20 years. She seems incredibly sad but resigned to it. How many wonderful creative people must there be in this world with similar stories? It makes me sad.

It's still a lovely hot 28 degrees here in Aix as Billy and I walk home from the bus stop. We stop on the way at the shaved ice stand and choose a flavour from one of 50 syrups, including mango, peach, citron, hazelnut, pear and even fairy-floss.

As we walk and slurp, Billy offhandedly says, "You know what, Mum? I quite like school now. I did find it difficult last week, especially because I don't speak much French, but I reckon I'll be able to handle it."

After a tough week, his words are as soothing as the cool shaved ice and offer instant relief.

Our New Home

Friday 17 September
Aix

"It is by chance that we met, by choice that we became friends." – *Unknown*

It's 6.30pm as I drive my little baby blue into the dusty car park opposite Billy's school and squeeze between a BMW and a Mercedes. Reluctantly I emerge from the car with my 'Made in Provence' rosé and French faire (cheese, olives and bread) piled precariously on a paper plate glamorously covered in cling wrap – grub more suited to an outback Australian picnic than a cocktail party. I consider it might be better to just turn up empty-handed and feign ignorance that I was asked to make a contribution.

Tottering down the gravel road flanked by fields of green, I hear the clink of glasses and the chatter of the well-to-do of France. I'm frankly a bit nervous. Will they all speak French? Will I be the only single mum there? Will they think I'm just one more woman on an *Under the Tuscan Sun* journey? I curse myself for my insecurities. It's really no business of mine what they think of me. I should just get over myself.

I inhale deeply, conjure up my best smile, open my heart and stick out my ample chest as I tiptoe up the steps to enter the vine-covered courtyard, the setting for the cocktail party. I appear to be the only one bearing food and the slick bow-tied waiters are serving canapés that have obviously been curated by a two-star Michelin restaurant.

Deftly I circle the crowd, sneak in the back way to the tables where the food is waiting to be dispensed and leave my embarrassing contribution on the table amongst the two-star Michelins. I sneak out of the room and make a beeline for the bar, desperate for something to get me relaxed and into my usual social chit-chatty state.

In no time I'm relaxed and introducing myself to some of the parents. As I return from the bar with my second drink, I stand there surveying the scene. That's when I notice her. She's beautiful and looks lonely sitting at the end of a table of English expats chattering away.

I approach the table and introduce myself. Her name is Florence. She's a single mum like me. Within minutes we're talking and giggling about all manner of topics, including unusual ways to meet men. We swap phone numbers. I drive home happy.

Our New Home

Saturday 18 September
Aix

"When I admire the wonder of a sunset or the beauty of the moon, my soul expands in worship of the creator." – Mahatma Gandhi

Saturdays in Aix are blissful. Billy is off having fun with his friends while I stroll around the clothing and jewellery markets, stop for coffee and visit the farmers markets to taste test, buy supplies and pick up my favourite pink and white oriental lilies.

Back home I hastily unpack the morning's purchases before meeting Susie and her husband, Bernie, who has now joined her in Aix, for lunch at a cute little Spanish place.

We're seated out the back in the courtyard with rambling vines overhead and an olive tree providing a little shade, as the steaming paella full of prawns, chicken, chorizo sausage and mussels is brought out with a cooling pitcher of sangria. The blend of spices, the delicious soupy stock and the textures of the meat and rice are a gastronomic delight. It's truly the best paella I've ever eaten.

The bright sun and the sangria make us all happy and drowsy, so there's no option but to head home for a little afternoon catnap. Nice.

I awake an hour later to Billy's insistent buzzing on the intercom. I let him in with his friend, Henry, and leave them to it while I grab my camera and go on my artist's date with myself.

I've decided to shoot some more of the buildings around town with interesting windows, signs and statues. I spend two hours walking around Aix, getting lost, with my eyes cast upwards looking for intriguing photo opportunities. I've always been a bit of a point-and-click photographer, but this time I take a more steadied artistic approach as I consider my subject, the colours, the angles and the light.

I stroll home with some great shots and a whole new respect for photographers who make a living from their art.

This evening's dinner is a fair-dinkum, home-made Aussie hamburger with chips to warm us both up for the world music festival – a festival dedicated to bringing alternative international music and installation artworks to the local community and hosted in a huge national park just outside Aix.

Now at the festival we're a bit perplexed. There are hardly any people here. The installation art is in a fenced off area and features discarded pieces of wood, boxes and old toilet seats surrounded by rubble backed by random slashings of paint on canvases. The rock band is as equally perplexing and not exciting either of us. Perhaps we're a little early for the main attractions?

We grab a drink and sit on the grass to enjoy the beautiful country setting and the pleasant warm evening breeze.

Then the best performance of the whole evening, one that is free and silent and totally unexpected, makes everything around us pale into significance – the sunset. As the sun sinks slowly behind the hills and the clouds drift and roll towards us, a brilliant colour, not quite pink and not quite orange, bursts across the sky. It illuminates everything around us.

After the sunset fades we agree that bed is a more enticing place to be. At home we sip our hot chocolates and review the exquisite photos we'd taken of our brilliant night sky and agree that the experience while not wholly satisfactory, was still worth every penny.

Sunday 19 September
Aix to Cassis

> "Right View; Right Intention; Right Speech; Right Action; Right Livelihood; Right Effort; Right Mindfulness; Right Concentration."
> – *The Noble Eightfold Path of Buddhism*

Today's pages bring up three words: *Book. Career. Love.*

I shelve the idea of a rant on my book and consider 'Career'. I don't really like the word. It's very corporate and linear and not at all suitable for artists. I recall 'Right Livelihood' is one of the Noble Eightfold Paths of Buddhism and decide to use that word from now on when referring to my future income.

So I write *Livelihood = Writing books and other creative projects.*

Now that other word. Love. A scary territory for me.

I carefully avoid a rant about James and write about John instead.

We met in a pub (as you do), nine years ago. He was my first lover after the end of my marriage. He was a fun, cheeky, intelligent, globetrotting Irish guy, living in England and travelling around Australia. He charmed me with stories of his freewheeling life and adventures, and his sharp wit and humour. I fell a little in love with him. But he was only staying in Sydney for that one week and we haven't seen each other since.

My friendship with John is based on a call from him, full of beer, every six months, from a pub in some exotic country, just to say hi or sometimes to ask me to marry him. Hilarious. It was always just a bit of fun for the two of us, nothing serious.

He knows we're in France and we've been regularly talking about catching up. Right now he's working on a property on the border of France and Switzerland, not far from us.

Even though I feel excited at the prospect of seeing him after all this time, I also feel unsure about it. Frankly, John is too much like James – full of charm and promises in no way backed by action, and a bit too wayward and elusive.

I end the pages with the hope to see John but if it's not meant to be, c'est la vie.

I head out the door for a jog with the music from 'So Frenchy So Chic' purring in my ears. It's a brilliant day and perfect for

Our New Home

our trip to Cassis, a fishing village on the coast about 30 minutes south of Aix and just east of Marseille.

Billy seems keener about today's event than last evening's and it doesn't require much bribing to get him out the door, especially as a boat trip and fish and chips are on the agenda.

I promise it's only 30 minutes away, according to the guidebook.

Two hours later we arrive in Cassis. There are three parties to blame – the French for putting up a highly inconvenient roadblock on the busiest day of the week, the Tom Tom for selecting the longest alternative route, and me for blindly trusting the Tom Tom and not pre-planning our trip.

So eventually we arrive in Cassis. It's a gorgeous village, surrounded by green rolling hills, vineyards and cliffs, and with a harbour filled with motorboats, yachts and fishing vessels of all shapes, sizes and colours. We walk down to Plage de la Grande Mere (Beach of the Great Sea) with its fine shell sand and stroll around the boardwalk till we find the promised fish and chips to satisfy our appetites.

A pleasant two hours on a boat ride around the Calanques of Cassis, the majestic inlets and limestone cliffs, tops off the day.

Some cliffs emerge straight, proud and unconquerable from the clear turquoise blue ocean below. Other smaller, more accessible cliffs are littered with spreadeagled humans, some clothed, some naked and soaking up the rays. Sailing boats are moored in every inlet while their passengers take a dip in the ocean before hauling themselves on-board for an aperitif.

It's our first time near the ocean since our final walk along Coogee beach over six weeks ago. It hurts just thinking about it but I don't say anything to Billy. I'm hoping he's not thinking about it too. We lick soothing gelati on our way back to the car and drive home. This time it takes 30 minutes.

Monday 20 September
Aix

"Adventure is just bad planning." – Roald Amundsen

One more week of French school before I get serious about writing again. With all the social occasions and so much to see and experience, and French school, it's been almost impossible to find the time to write. As much as I adore writing, I'm not the kind that can just write for an hour here and there. I need hours of uninterrupted time to get in flow and write with purpose.

So I forget about writing and practise being fully present with Billy as we eat breakfast to the accompanying church bells, talk about the day ahead and head off to our respective schools.

Our New Home

Tonight our lovely new neighbours, Susie and Bernie, are hosting us for dinner.

I've cooked more dinners in the past 20 days than I've cooked in the past 20 weeks. Billy has been regularly encouraging me with comments like, "Mum, you're actually becoming not a bad cook." Not exactly a standing ovation, but nice.

It's easier to be a good cook, or at least a better one, here in Aix. Firstly, the produce here is bountiful and accessible every day and, secondly, I've had time to cook. In Sydney, after a full day of work, school pick-up, homework supervision, dog walking and the rest, cooking was the last thing I wanted to do. It was a chore rather than a relaxant.

That said, even if my cooking has improved, I still prefer eating food lovingly prepared by someone with a more creative culinary repertoire than mine. So I'm excited about tonight's dinner upstairs with Susie and Bernie.

We're greeted with a glass of rosé and a Coke and we share a delectable antipasto plate, followed by the best-ever bouillabaisse – a delicious traditional Provençale fish stew originating in Marseille.

After dinner Billy reads the story he's written for English, a Cluedo-inspired essay entitled 'The Ruby Red Shoe'. All three of us are mesmerised by his words and left wanting more as he ends. I'm biased, obviously, but think he has a real talent for writing.

I've been encouraging him to write about his journey in France and contribute to our blog, but he's more interested in Facebooking, Skyping and watching YouTube clips when he gets anywhere near the computer. I'm hoping Susie and Bernie's enthusiastic response will inspire him to write more than his nagging mother.

Billy pops back downstairs to our apartment to bed and the conversation gets louder as the wine keeps flowing. We discuss our respective forthcoming trips to Italy. Susie and Bernie are seasoned travellers and have lots of travelling tips to share.

I'd been seriously considering a road trip in our little baby blue but after yesterday's outing to Cassis I'm not so sure so am considering a train journey.

Then Bernie makes me laugh out loud.

"Whether you drive or go by train, I only have one thing to say – be mindful of the seven Ps: Proper Prior Planning Prevents Piss Poor Performance."

Perfect advice for me.

It's late when I go back downstairs. Billy is fast asleep and I give him a kiss goodnight and hop into my bed, mellow and happy.

⚜ ⚜ ⚜

Tuesday 21 September
Aix

"Alcohol may be man's worst enemy, but the Bible says love your enemy." – Frank Sinatra

Our New Home

God, I wish I hadn't drunk so much last night. Today I feel ill and tired and annoyed at myself. I just want to curl up and go back to sleep.

I scrawl these words, bleary-eyed. Before leaving Sydney I'd made a promise, to myself and Grace, that I'd change my drinking habits while here in France. Although I don't drink heavily every day, I've often used alcohol as a crutch, particularly in times of stress and loneliness.

Drinking in a state of negative emotion, and particularly on my own, is a habit I want to kick. I just want to drink when I'm happy and in the company of friends, and limit the amount I consume.

So, today I'm annoyed at myself. I've really been drinking very little since being here, but last night I drank two glasses too many and now I'm suffering.

I vent for the rest of the morning pages about it and make a decision I'm going to play hooky today. Ironic that I'd booked a wine-tasting course this afternoon, too. Guess I won't be going to that, either!

I get Billy off to school and crawl back into bed and pull the doona over my head. It's been a long time since I've done this. I'm usually up bright and early and getting into the day. I feel guilty about it, for at least 10 minutes, anyway. But then I have a blissful day sleeping and reading, and even writing for a while, until Billy comes home.

It's about 7pm and the phone rings. It's John, the Irishman. We chat and laugh for a while and he says he really, really wants to see me. He then asks to speak to Billy. I hand the phone over and they chat while I cook dinner.

I can tell by Billy's tone that he likes him. I really like John too, and feel it would be a great shame if we don't get to see each other.

Wednesday 22 September
Aix

"No man is worth your tears, and when you find the man who is, he won't make you cry." – *Unknown*

I've been thinking about men and relationships, and decide to write down the qualities I'd like in a man in my morning pages.

I'd like a man who is honest, steady, clear-minded, able to set boundaries, spiritual, capable of deep emotion, intimate, compassionate, caring, considerate, intelligent, humorous, humble, trustworthy, monogamous, loves Billy, has kids, creative, happy, fit and healthy, financially healthy, loves his family, has lots of friends, adventurous, moderately handsome…

I abruptly stop writing. Bloody hell, that's a tall order! I go through each word and consider whether I, myself, possess these qualities. Some, yes. Some, no. And some more than others at different times.

Hmmm. Maybe these are the very qualities I should be cultivating in myself before I seek them in someone else?

I recall the conversation I'd had with Julie just last week, about her new boyfriend, Marc.

"You know, Carolyn," she'd said in her characteristically animated way, "I just asked the universe for a man who'll show up for me, and that's what I got."

Our New Home

That's a pretty good summary, really. I'd like a man who will support me and be there for me, who'll just show up. The rest is negotiable.

I recall each of the men who've graced my life and I can honestly say there was only ever a couple that really showed up for me, and it definitely wasn't James or John.

Okay, so now I'm starting to think, while I might not be ready for a relationship, it might be fun to at least have a French flirtation. Every time one of my girlfriends or sisters rings, the first question I get is whether I've met any hot French men yet.

So how does one go about actually meeting a French man, who happens to speak English, in this city? I ponder the options. I could join a French dating website. I could go to a bar. I could ask my friends to introduce me to some. I could put an ad on the notice board in Book in Bar. Bingo. That's it. I jump out of bed, grab a piece of green card and a glittery silver pen and write an ad: *Fun, outgoing, 46-year-old Australian woman, here until December and seeking French/English conversation with French man. Call Carolyn...*

I'm tempted to write "conversation and flirtation" but I don't. It already reads like a bad singles ad.

This all takes place before 7am and with only six hours sleep. There's a glint in my eye as Billy and I get ready for school and go our separate ways. After school I hurry to Book in Bar, stick my ad on the big notice board and check the other ads to see if there are any possibilities. Alas, there are none.

When I arrive home, Billy is there all set up for the afternoon. He has a baguette and a citron meringue pie lined up with a big glass of orange juice, his books and pencil case on one side, and the computer on the other. I'm not sure which is getting the most attention – the food, Facebook or French homework. Whatever. He looks as happy as Larry.

Thursday 23 September
Aix

"God heals, and the doctor takes the fee."
– Benjamin Franklin

It's very early and I can't sleep so I jump into my morning pages. As my pen scrawls across the page like an agitated spider, I think how embarrassed I'd be if someone else were to read these pages. After about 20 lines I stop and do a little meditation for some inspiration. I end the pages without judgement and gratitude for the day ahead.

For now it's time to rise and be of service to Billy. Bath. Breakfast. Bus.

He's gone and I'm off to school too. This morning we're required to give a speech (in French, of course) on how we usually spend

Our New Home

Sundays at home in our own country. Of course I can only talk about our old life in Coogee with Dash and at Nippers as I've no idea what our future life will be like in Melbourne.

It's my turn. (In French.) "On Sunday mornings in Sydney Australia I arise early and take our dog Dash for a walk. Billy and I then walk to Coogee beach to participate in Nippers. We belong to the Coogee Surf Life Saving Club where we learn how to rescue people from the surf…" I unexpectedly choke up as I say it. The realisation that we're caught in a hiatus between two lives hits home. There's a real moment of sadness. What if our new Sundays are never going to be as good as our old Sundays?

As I leave school, Billy rings.

"Mum, I'm in the sickroom and there's blood gushing out of my chin. I tripped over a soccer ball and smashed my chin on a stone. I need stitches. Can you come and get me?"

He's very wobbly and quite pale when I get to him. I want to hug him but that would be totally uncool. Half an hour later we're with our friendly, handsome French doctor who gently cleans his wound and inspects it.

It turns out that stitches are not required, just a plaster to keep the skin pulled together until it heals, and a tetanus injection.

"He'll have a scar," the doctor says.

"Girls love the rugged look – it'll be a great reminder of your time in France," I reassure Billy as we leave.

He doesn't look so convinced.

Billy is understandably subdued all afternoon at home. He just rests and eats the fridge bare until dinner. At least the accident hasn't affected his appetite.

After a delicious chicken curry made with Indian spices from the markets, and more compliments on how my cooking is improving from Billy, my friend Nadine from French school drops over for a drink.

Nadine is from Karlsruhe, Allemagne (Germany). We get out my map of Europe and she tells me about her hometown and her country, and we discuss all the places we've been and that are still on our bucket list.

I hesitantly pull out the Pastis bottle. I'd read about the famous French liqueur in Peter Mayle's books so had decided a few days ago to buy a bottle and try it. Pastis has often been associated with its outlawed predecessor absinthe, and is distilled from star anise with added liquorice-root and bottled with sugar.

I'd opened the bottle and poured myself a finger width. One sip had nearly made my eyes pop out. With an alcoholic content of 45-50 per cent and its pungent flavour, I was pretty sure it would never touch my lips again.

With some further research I'd discovered that it's best served with water and ice, which turns it cloudy (and, hopefully, drinkable). Nadine loves it, and I reckon it's not too bad now either. Maybe I could be converted.

It's 11pm and I'm in bed. The phone rings. It's John. He sounds a little weird, like he's had a few drinks.

"What are you looking for in a relationship?" he asks. Pretty deep stuff at this hour of the night and I'm not really prepared to answer that question out of the blue, so without thinking I say, "Nothing, right now. I'm here to heal from my last sad relationship not start a new one."

Then I recall my conversation with Julie and say, "You

know what, can I retract that? I just want a man that shows up for me."

I'm not sure what the point of all his questions are and I'm amused at the depth of our conversation.

"Do you still want to see me?" he asks.

"Sure," I say, with complete uncertainty.

Friday 24 September
Aix

"Thinking is easy, acting is difficult, and to put one's thoughts into action is the most difficult thing in the world." – Johann Wolfgang Goethe

I write in my morning pages all the things I like about John and then the things that concern me about him and his past behaviours. I decide I don't really know him, actually, which makes me keener to see him, of course. So I muster up all my courage and decide to take matters into my own hands.

I ask Billy how he'd feel about a road trip. He says fine, as long as there's internet access wherever we're going. Priceless.

It's 7.30am. I call John to get his voicemail and leave a

message: "Billy and I are keen to drive up and see you this weekend. What do you think? Can you call me please?"

It's the last morning of French school. I've learnt just enough to get me by and made some nice friends. I consider registering for another course but decide against it. Frankly, my spiritual and creative recovery and my writing are more important to me. I just don't have the brain space to learn a language proficiently and write a book simultaneously.

Almost everyone in the class is going back to their home country in the next few days so we share a nice lunch together before swapping contact details and bidding each other au revoir.

It's mid afternoon before I hear from John, who says it's not possible for us to stay with him because he's renovating the house there and it's a mess. He suggests maybe meeting halfway somewhere tomorrow.

It's all very noncommittal and vague, but I agree and ask if he has any ideas about where. "No, let me think about it and get back to you in an hour or two," he says.

Billy and I have yet another gourmet dinner prepared by me and we spend time watching downloads on the computer before going to bed.

I turn the light out late, with not a call or text from John. Okay, so I'd called his bluff. Not a new experience with him. I feel a little abandoned and lonely, but let it go. It's not like I haven't got anything better to do. It would've just been intriguing to see if there was any spark after all these years. But I guess it's not to be.

Our New Home

Saturday 25 September
Aix en Provence to Aix les Bains

"To me... music exists to elevate us as far as possible above everyday life." – Gabriel Faure

I leave Billy for a sleep in as I head off on a run with my latest musical discovery, Lisa Mitchell, a young folk and rock singer from Albury NSW. I've been discovering new artists almost daily here, courtesy of iTunes. I've always loved music, but admittedly my appetite for it had diminished somewhat, mainly due to time. Now I have the time and heart for it again, I've been hungrily exploring new artists and old ones I've never heard before.

My music taste is changing and I'm enjoying the music of lesser-known and more alternative indie artists. As I run I don't just listen to the music, I feel it throughout my body. The lyrics, the music and the space between every line combine to inspire every step. And now I'm also singing. Are these the tell tale signs of spiritual recovery?

If I could have just one other real creative interest other than writing, it would probably be singing. I tried singing lessons about 18 months ago, but I gave it up after six lessons. It wasn't that I didn't have the voice for it. My problem was that the words would get caught in my throat along with my emotions and I couldn't go deep enough to belt out the tune with emotion. I was afraid that if I dug too deep, I'd collapse into a sobbing mess.

It was a time when I was particularly torn up about James and it really didn't help that I was attempting to sing Leonard Cohen's 'Hallelujah', either. So rather than use singing as a therapy to break through it and out, I gave it up. I was just too petrified to go there.

I'm just a couple of kilometres into my run when a text comes through.

"You still up for it?"

So typical of John. I'm annoyed and I definitely don't really feel 'up for it', especially as his text just disturbed my brilliant run. Now I can't concentrate on the music or my run and I stop to sit on a park bench and think about what I should do.

I'd given up on the idea of visiting him when I turned my light out last night. I'm tempted to just ignore the text, but then I consider it. If we see each other, we'll put an end to this little fantasy we've both kept up for nine years. It will be over.

I finish my run and text back "Sure".

He calls me within five seconds. "Let's meet at Aix les Bains, halfway between us both, around 4pm this afternoon. We'll find a hotel when we get there."

Am I stupid or what? Maybe I shouldn't be doing this with my son in tow? I roll in the door hot and sweaty from my run to tell Billy the plan. He seems okay about it, as long as the hotel has the internet, as promised. Within an hour, we're in the little baby blue and ready to go.

Our New Home

The drive is uneventful (apart from negotiating the road tolls) and Billy and I chat on and off, in between him dozing. The poor kid still has a plaster on his chin and he's itching to take it off.

The views are breathtaking and the landscape turns more mountainous and Swiss-like as we pass through big tunnels carved right through the middle of the mountains. It's also getting much colder and I could kick myself for not wearing my boots.

The closer we get, the more nervous I become. I already know John's pretty much the same on the inside as we've spent many an hour talking over the years. But will he still look the same? Will he be fat or thin? Will he have lost all his hair? I haven't seen even a photo of him in nine years.

We arrive in Aix les Bains, which is not far from Geneva, and I call John. He's already there and has found a hotel and booked a room for Billy and I and another for him.

We drive in to the car park. I can feel my heart beating and Billy is laughing at me.

"Mum," he says, "I can tell you're nervous. Who is this bloke, anyway?"

His comment makes me laugh and relieves my anxiety. "He's just an old friend I met in Sydney years ago."

John walks up to the car and we hug and surreptitiously check each other out. It's so weird seeing this man who was my first ever lover after my marriage. He looks exactly the same as he did nine years ago.

Within minutes we're checked in and sitting at one of the few okay-enough drinking holes in this town – a town that doesn't appear to have too many redeeming features on this very cold afternoon.

We enjoy a drink or two and a walk around the town. Billy turns a bit surly. Maybe he's feeling threatened by this man who's arrived from nowhere. He makes it clear he'd prefer to be in the hotel room on his computer than having dinner with us, so we escort him back to the room with dinner in hand. I feel like a neglectful mother and guilty for putting my own needs before his by coming here. John and I consume a five-cheese fondue at a nearby restaurant as we drink wine and chat and laugh about absolutely everything.

It seems like no topic is taboo between us and we just talk and talk. I still feel a little attracted to him after all these years.

On the way back to the hotel we don't touch, we don't hold hands, we don't walk arm in arm. Nothing. I'm not going to instigate anything romantic and neither, it seems, is he. We get back to the floor our rooms are on. We stop to say goodnight. He gives me a tentative kiss on the cheek. That's it. Nothing else. In bed, with Billy snoring away in the bed beside me, I feel incredibly sad and lonely. I've no idea exactly why. Maybe it has everything to do with my history around men, or just maybe the fantasy was preferable to the reality?

Our New Home

Sunday 26 September
Aix les Bains to Aix en Provence

"Gain and loss, birth and death are in the hands of God."
— Sri Sathya Sai Baba

For the first time since being here, I don't write my morning pages. I just can't write. I feel blocked and numb.

I'm sad and confused about last night and feel totally rejected and unattractive. Consciously I'd told myself I didn't want anything to happen, but maybe subconsciously I was hoping something would.

We meet John for breakfast. I'm pleasant but distant. Billy is tired and grumpy. John is subdued and distracted. It's all pretty awkward and I can't wait to escape and drive home so I can be with my own thoughts while Billy sleeps. Soon enough it's over. We say goodbye with a bland kiss on each other's cheeks and wave each other farewell.

I drive home with intense focus, weighing up the whole crazy evening and everything that he said and I said and what had transpired. We arrive home safely, both dog tired. I go into robot mode, doing what needs to be done, cooking dinner, organising Billy for school the next day and getting him to bed.

I give him an extra big hug and thank him for indulging me and accompanying me on this trip. When I'm sure he's fast asleep, I collapse into bed and weep.

⚜ ⚜ ⚜

Monday 27 September
Aix

"Art is a man's nature; nature is God's art."
– Philip James Bailey

I wake up feeling surprisingly calm and peaceful. Last night's grief had nothing to do with John and everything to do with me. It felt like a final letting go of sorts.

I lay completely still, willing myself into a state of deep meditation, breathing deeply and allowing the air to fill my lungs. I visualise myself holding a bunch of brightly coloured helium-filled balloons, each adorned with the face of the past men in my life.

One by one I release the balloons, starting with the men in my distant memory and finishing with John and finally James. I give gratitude to each one for their presence in my life and wish them love. When they're all released

Our New Home

I feel immense relief and smile to myself at this childlike cord-cutting ceremony.

The symbolism of the weekend and this simple ceremony provide an incessant stream of content for the morning pages.

After Billy is off to school I stroll to the park, this time without music spurring me on. I walk in a meditative and contemplative state, listening to the cawing crows, the ducks quacking and the school children squealing with delight. I sit on a hefty boulder and turn my face and my heart towards the sun and go into a deep meditation. As I transition out of the meditation, my gaze turns downwards to the gurgling creek just feet away. I cast a handful of fallen leaves from the nearby plane trees into the clear water one by one. I feel totally present, like I'm an integral part of nature, not separate to it.

I dawdle dreamily in the direction of home to pick up my daily delicacies from the markets before enjoying a simple brunch. Oh, if only life could start like this every day for everybody, what a world we would live in.

The weekend's events are brilliant motivation for my writing. It's midday when I begin and I only stop when Billy comes home nearly six hours later.

Tuesday 28 September
Aix

Om Om Om
Om namah shivaya gurave
Sat chit ananda murtaye
Nichprapanchaya shantaya
Niralambaya tejase
Om

I start my morning pages with a bit of sadness today. Despite the cord-cutting ceremony of yesterday I'm still a bit confused and sad about the weekend's events. There's been no text and no phone call from John. Nothing. I wonder what he's feeling about it all. It would be nice to have an honest conversation and a laugh about it with him. But maybe no contact is the best option for a while.

We start my first yoga class here in Aix with this beautiful chant. "I welcome the presence of Shiva, the universe. In truth, consciousness and bliss. Never absent and always peaceful, perfectly free and light."

I love yoga and have practised it for years, although not always that diligently. Like many of my other healthy practices, yoga had fallen by the wayside in Sydney.

Somehow it seems even more spiritual and special here in this beautiful city of Aix as Elise our teacher gently imparts

Our New Home

her teachings in Frenglish 'Orientès vers le bas chien' (downward facing dog), 'repsirer' (breathe in) 'expirer' (breathe out). I love every minute of this yoga class and commit to a 12-week program before leaving.

On the way home I sit in a café and sip an espresso, indulge in some people watching and listen to the chatter of the vendors and their customers at the markets just metres away. The beautiful French accents mingle with the myriad smells coming my way as I fill three pages of my journal until I've nothing left to write.

At home I continue to write, this time on my computer. It's a different kind of writing, unlike journalling where the words come from my stream of unconsciousness.

I give thought to the words I use and the structure of the sentences. The sentences flow into paragraphs and the paragraphs flow into pages and before I know it, the bell is buzzing and Billy is home.

I've no idea how good or bad my writing is. I remind myself that my job is to just do the work, not judge it. My job is to focus on the quantity, not the quality, and the content, not the outcome. My job is to just show up at the page, do what I love and what makes me happy.

Billy is really happy tonight as he eats my French/Australian made-up stew-like concoction with rice (definitely not à la Julia Child). He's quite animated as he tells me all the gossip about his friends at school – the boys and a few girls he likes and hangs out with.

I'm so grateful that he's settling in and starting to enjoy this experience. I can already see how much it's maturing him. It's becoming an education in life in every way.

Wednesday 29 September
Aix

"Every sense hath been o'erstrung, and each frail fibre of the brain sent forth her thoughts all wild and wide." – Lord Byron

Billy has gone to school and I'm having a totally self-indulgent sense-filled day. I start it with a run around Parc de la Torse listening to Lloyd Cole (and the Commotions), UK singer and songwriter. At home I take a beautiful long bath filled with olive oil essences and bubbles and gaze out of the window at the tree and blue sky behind it while listening to a single bird chirp and a dog bark in the distance. I'm humming to the music of Sade, the beautiful Nigerian-born singer who's been a favourite since my early 20s.

When I emerge from the bath, I moisturise my body from head to toe with my gorgeous vanilla-scented body lotion, make myself up and dry my hair with tenderness and self-love. I slip on a summery dress, my most favourite jewels and strap on some sandals.

"I feel beautiful and I look beautiful," I say to myself before I walk out the door.

I'm off to see the movie *Eat, Pray, Love* in French and on my own. I first read the book when I was on a retreat in Desert Hot Springs in California over two years ago. I'd read it once

Our New Home

more since then and loved it.

I'm pretty sceptical about the movie though, as I'm not a huge fan of Julia Roberts and I'm not sure if the book can really be captured adequately on screen. I'm thrilled about seeing it in French even without English sub-titles.

So into the darkness of the cinema I retreat, alone yet feeling indescribably happy. I immerse myself in the movie with all its glorious imagery of Italy, India and Indonesia, and the human angst and life jumping out at me. I barely understand a word of it but it really doesn't matter.

Now it's time to activate my taste buds at lunch with more friends from French school – Andrew and Elizabeth are a wonderful Canadian couple also on an extended stay in Aix, Lucia is my lovely Italian friend who lives in Aix with her husband, and there's Therese from Germany.

We sit outdoors at a restaurant on Place des Cardeurs sipping a yummy rosé and eating thin slivers of duck and pear abreast a delicate salad covered with a light mustard dressing.

We're telling stories and not attempting to speak one word of French. Um, bad, I'm thinking (for just a second). The conversation is lively and fun, and more punchy and engaging in English than my faltering French. It's a fun afternoon, until I excuse myself all of a sudden for my next appointment – a massage. It's an essential way to finish my day of pure indulgence and get that last vital sense – touch, stimulated.

When Billy arrives home, he finds his mother purring and sleepy, like a contented cat. He consumes the after-school delicacies he's becoming so used to in five minutes flat while I help him with his homework as best I can.

We eat dinner and watch *Modern Family* and *How I Met Your Mother*. We giggle at them both and talk about which characters we like best and why. We're connected, my son and I. He falls asleep in his bed and I kiss him goodnight before hopping into my own bed for yet another love of my life, reading. Life really doesn't get much better than this.

⚜ ⚜ ⚜

Thursday 30 September

Aix

"You've got to dance like nobody is watching and love like it's never going to hurt." – Unknown

The other morning I'd been brainstorming some classes I'd love to do. I'd come up with dancing, singing, photography, sculpting and real-life drawing. Next to dancing I'd scribbled down 'Zumba' (a fitness class fusing Latin rhythms with dance steps and high-energy moves). Being a girl of action, I'd found a local class and managed to cajole Lucia into coming along with me.

As we arrive, a gorgeous hot French man, who is obviously our instructor, also arrives. I decide it's totally worth coming,

Our New Home

even if I'm really, really bad at Zumba. Then all the gorgeous young stick-thin, flexible French girls turn up. I guess most of them are half my age, and that they know every step.

We take a position at the back of the room close to the door where we can escape if we need and where I can't see myself in the mirror. The music starts and the class begins. The instructor is very kindly using his best Frenglish just for us. I can't follow the steps for peanuts, but I'm having a hell of a great time laughing at myself and Lucia jiving away beside me.

One hour later we finish. We're both sweating and laughing and feeling like complete idiots. And neither of us care, one little bit.

Billy comes home happy. It was sports day today and his soccer and basketball team were victorious. We have a French lesson with our new tutor, Nathalie, before we head upstairs for cocktail hour with Laura and Marc, our landlords.

Marc gives us a fascinating history lesson on Aix en Provence and Laura gives us an impromptu French lesson. They're very kind and hospitable.

It's our last night in 18 Rue Cardinale, the place we've made our home for the past month. We're both sad at leaving. We've loved this place; the thrill of opening the big French windows every morning and looking down our street; the gentle rhythmic toll of the church bells; the whirr of the engine of the little tourist train that passes by regularly each day; the deep bath; the art on all the walls; the light, airy, Frenchy feel of the whole place.

We're moving to a new place in Aix, right next to the Hotel Deville – an earthy, arty apartment on the top floor of a block of apartments.

So now, after dinner, I pack up all our belongings in this lovely place. I'm amazed at how much we've amassed in just one month.

Billy is in bed fast asleep and I'm sitting up in bed checking my emails. There are a few from friends and family, and I start to feel a pang of homesickness. I wonder how Dash is and what's happening in Coogee. And that's when I think about James.

I haven't thought about him for days. I wonder how he is and if he's happy and if he even thinks about me. Then, for some inexplicable reason, I draft him an email.

'I hope this note finds you well and happy. Billy and I are having a great time in Aix and although it took us a little while to settle in, it's already feeling like home. The language barrier can be challenging so we're having private lessons. I finished my French course last week and am now spending my time exercising, making friends and writing lots. Billy is enjoying school and making lots of friends. I think of you often and hope you're okay. Take care of yourself and keep in touch. Love Carolyn and Billy'

I hit the send button before I give it a second thought. I don't know if he'll respond. I'm guessing not. I know that I didn't send it to get a response, anyway. I sent it to let him know I've forgiven him, that I'm healing and that I'm moving on. I hope it's received with love and forgiveness for me too.

Our New Home

Friday 1 October
Aix to Ventabren

"To live a creative life, we must lose our fear of being wrong." – Innerspace

I open to a new blank white page in my journal and feel a little thrill that it will soon be filled with words. Whether those words will be intelligent and thoughtful does not concern me. My job is to just fill the page, then fill two more.

I recall a comment Billy had made yesterday.

"Mum, you know how you want me to travel after school and Dad wants me to go to uni, why don't I do both and come to uni in France?"

I write about the wisdom of my son and how this experience might shape his future. Then for some inexplicable reason my writings turn negative and I rant about all the ways I'm not a good mother.

I nag him too much. I try to control him. I don't always listen to him. I let him spend too much time on his computer.

And on and on it goes. I end the pages feeling like crap. I don't judge it or reread it. I just snap the book shut and get out of bed.

I bid farewell to Laura. With everything we own stowed in the back of the baby blue I drive down Rue Cardinale to visit a village or two before I pick up Billy from school. It's a gorgeous day as I explore Le Tholonet, a favourite place for Cézanne with its magnificent views to Mount Saint-Victoire, and drive through Chateauneuf-Le-Rouge, Rousset, Meyreuil and on to Gardanne, the capital of the Provence coal basin with its smokestacks dominating the horizon, and then into Bouc-Bel-Air.

And that's when it happens. I'm driving around the winding, narrow cobble-stoned roads lined with ancient homes stacked neatly together, when I realise the road is more suitable for pedestrians than vehicles. I find myself at a juncture, in more ways than one, with the houses on both sides only inches away. My only options are to turn an impossible sharp right, down a steep hill, or reverse back from whence I came.

I wish I'd paid extra for insurance and I hope no one is watching from behind all those quaint curtained windows.

I stop the car to get out and assess the situation. With the handbrake on, I open my door as wide as I can to squeeze out. As I do, the car lurches forward. I've no option but to jump back in and descend the hill. The sound of the car scraping against the wall makes me shudder and scream before I finally grind to a halt at the bottom of the hill.

I get out shaking from head to toe. A toothless laughing old lady asks, "Ça va? Ça va?"

"Oui, oui, merci," I respond as I inspect the damage and she shuffles off cackling to herself.

Back in the car, I hit the steering wheel with fury at my spectacular display of incompetence.

A few hours later, after I've collected Billy from school, I calm down and manage a smile. At least no one was hurt and I have a funny (although expensive) story to tell.

Our New Home

We drive to Ventabren, a village West of Aix with a small population and dominated by the ruins of a castle, Queen Joanna. We're staying a night with Chiara and Claudio, the new landlords of our apartment in Aix. They're Italian and have lived in Aix for 20 years.

We arrive to be greeted by Chiara and Babette, her fluffy white dog, and trek into the village to their amazing 17th-century home. We walk up to the pinnacle of the village to the cemetery with its exquisite views over the rolling vineyards and olive orchards.

As we walk, Chiara tells us lively stories about the village and its inhabitants. She's a funny, multi-dimensional, intelligent and engaging woman, in her own brusque-but-warm Italian way. I love her and so does Billy.

We dine with Richard (a fellow Australian), Nicole, Claudio and Chiara. The wine stimulates the tastebuds, the conversation and the laughter as we indulge in seafood marinara, salads, cheeses and a fig flan, with Moët et Chandon on the side. Is there no end to the hospitality being bestowed upon us in this wonderful country?

On my way to bed I bask in the aura of this eccentric home filled with paintings, books, musical instruments, objects d'art, eclectic furnishings, creativity, love and memories. As I close my eyes I say a little artist's prayer reaffirming my commitment to a more creative home and daily life in Melbourne.

Saturday 2 October
Ventabren to Aix

> "Be grateful for the home you have, knowing that at this moment, all you have is all you need."
> – Sarah Ban Breathnach

I wake up with my son snoring in my ear in the bed next to me. He's not making a move as I sit up and turn the light on to write my morning pages. I write about how grateful I am to be having this experience with Billy, how much I love Aix, the generosity of the people we've met, how grateful I am to be gently recovering my creativity, my spirituality and my self-love and self-respect.

After kissing the baby blue goodbye and returning her to the rental company for some tender loving repairs we share the plat du jour of poisson tartar and frites (raw dollard fish and chips) with Chiara and Claudio at one of their favourite restaurants in Aix.

After lunch we unload our belongings on the street at the stairs of 6 Rue Paul Bert, the address of our new apartment. It's just 50 metres away from Place de la Mairie, the farmers markets and all manner of figure-enhancing food outlets. We trudge up four flights of stairs and enter what will be our new home for the next three months. I feel instantly connected and at home.

Our New Home

It has a bedroom for me, and a cosy loft with a big bed for Billy that overlooks the living area. The warm terracotta tiled floor is adorned with a huge plush orange sofa and a bright striped rug under an old leather inlaid coffee table. And there's a little red desk, the perfect surface upon which I intend to finish my book.

The kitchen is a stainless steel and light wood affair and complements the wood trestle table with mismatched chairs and the exposed beams and old wood stove. There are vines creeping along the beams and it's filled with light and sun. And the coup de grâce? 360-degree views over the town of Aix to Mount Saint-Victoire from the rooftop balcony.

It's the most perfect writer's retreat any writer could hope for!

The afternoon is spent stocking our new home with food, flowers and our few belongings. By dinner we're settled in and 100 per cent at home. I marvel at how little I really do need to be happy – my son, my health, a few clothes, some yummy food, a roof over our head, a hot shower, my music, my books, my computer, my writing and a handful of lovely friends.

Why do we Westerners complicate our lives in the relentless pursuit of material possessions?

Sunday 3 October

Aix

> "The music that really turns me on is either running toward God or away from God. Both recognise the pivot, that God is at the center of the jaunt." – *Bono*

I'm running towards God, my Higher Power, today, as I enter Parc de la Torse with my old favourite, Natalie Merchant, serenading me.

After a lovely lunch with my son, I grab my camera and walk down Cours Mirabeau for a music and dance feast. Six boot-scooting line dancers dressed in black cowboy outfits entertain the crowd with their perfectly timed dance routine while a latino band plays to an adoring, hip-swaying audience and a gaggle of dreadlocked youths play gypsy music on an assortment of unidentifiable instruments.

It's so heart-warming to see both musicians and audience so connected, uninhibited and into the music and life.

When I arrive home, Billy and I listen to music all afternoon, sometimes his, sometimes mine.

He plays on his computer while I set an action plan to seriously start writing tomorrow. There's no getting out of it now. I have my little red writing desk set up in our artist's retreat and no distractions in the week ahead. I just pray that I'll be able to untap my creative writing vein again.

Our New Home

Monday 4 October

Aix

"Writing is the only thing, that when I do it, I don't feel like I should be doing something else." – Gloria Steinem

It's 7.45am. Billy has left for school. For no identifiable reason, I'm a little flat as I write my morning pages.

I feel lost. I don't know what I'll do when we leave France and return to Melbourne. In Sydney, I was stuck but at least we had a home, a dog, friends, a routine and a certain structure to life. In my pursuit of freedom, I've thrown everything away and now I have no anchor…

For a whole page I blurt out my fears. Then at the top of the second page I write, *Get over yourself. Be grateful.*

I spend the rest of the pages writing about every little thing I'm grateful for in my life. I end it with: *I'm grateful for my anchor, my writing.*

After a lovely, long, rhythmic swim at the local pool and breakfast, I close down every application on my computer except Word and iTunes and put on Damien Rice, Irish singer songwriter and talented instrumentalist.

I forget the month, the day, the hour, the minute and even the second I'm currently in, as I cast my mind back in time. I write with a fever. I forget to eat, to drink, to pee. 2109 words later I get up as Billy rings the buzzer to get in.

The sky is settling like a big pink, warm, fluffy blanket over Aix this evening. I sit on the balcony with an aperitif while the dinner is simmering and Billy is doing his homework. I take photo after photo of the rooftops with their wonky, bright orange chimneystacks, the majestic church spires, the imposing Mount Saint-Victoire and the little birds chattering away happily to each other while balancing precariously on overhead wires. It warms the heart, this view.

I'm delighted tonight because Billy has invited me for a rendezvous to watch *Chocolat*, a movie he's studying in French, which happens to be one of my favourite ever movies. He figures if he sees it in English too it will help him with his French and who am I to argue? It's a night of total tranquilité in every way.

⚜ ⚜ ⚜

Tuesday 5 October
Aix

"Life is never easy for those who dream."
– Robert James Weller

Our New Home

The fine and intimate details of the highly erotic dream I'd had about James come floating back to me as I awake from my sleep. I'm instantly surly and annoyed.

Why can't he just f**k off. I've done everything physically possible to eliminate this man from my life and he still occupies my mind and now he's coming back to me in my dreams. What else do I need to do?

I cry to whoever is listening up there. I recall Grace's words: "Carolyn, you need to heal from your addiction to him. It will take time. Be patient." I remind myself that it's less than two months since I last saw James. What do I expect? Instant erasure?

Yoga is my elixir. I hum out my "Oms" with depth and feeling, and allow my steady breathing to take me deep into my practice. I leave feeling wonderfully limber, light and peaceful, ready to write and write and write. And that's exactly what I do all day.

Wednesday 6 October
Aix

"Technology is a queer thing… it brings you great gifts with one hand, and it stabs you in the back with the other." – Carrie P Snow

Today is the day Billy gets his own computer – and we both get peace and independence.

I'm not 100 per cent sure it's a good thing. Billy loves his technology a little too much, like many teenage boys, I guess. It's his link to home and the outside world and his entertainment system all in one.

With no TV, no after-school sports and not much else to do after homework and dinner, the computer is his first option. I wish he'd pick up a book, a sketchpad or write a story or respond with a "yes" to my invitation to play chess or cards, but he doesn't. He loves technology.

And then I beat myself up because I don't know how to manage his use without us having a major argument. So I let it go because it makes him happy. If he was surly, unsociable and uncommunicative I would worry even more, but he's not. He's an engaging, likeable and friendly young man, or so everyone tells me. Nagging and prohibition would do nothing. And anyway, who am I to talk? I don't know how I'd survive without my computer either.

He walks in the door and I bring out the box. He's pretty excited. Within minutes he has it configured and working. The smile on his face melts any apprehension I have, for now anyway.

Our New Home

Thursday 7 October

Aix

"Pray and let God worry." – *Martin Luther King*

This morning I'm writing my own artist's prayer. I've bought a gorgeous new pen just for the occasion. I flick to the back of my journal, close my eyes for five minutes and breathe deeply before I write.

> *God give me the grace to heal myself, to grow personally and spiritually without the need for immediate closure.*
>
> *God give me the grace to be patient with myself and not rush to a decision over my future livelihood.*
>
> *God give me the grace to enjoy the small things in life: the sun, the chatter of people, the food, the coffee, the park, the arts.*
>
> *God give me the grace to pursue a creative life and build a creative home.*
>
> *God give me the grace to have patience with my son and let go of control.*
>
> *God give me the grace to manage my money wisely and be free of worry.*

God give me the grace to write my book to heal myself and help heal others.

God give me the grace to continue being fit and healthy.

God give me the grace to love with all my heart and soul.

God give me the grace to be open to every opportunity, offer and invitation.

God give me the grace to say no, when I really don't want something.

God give me the grace to give to others and show compassion.

God give me the grace to use my instinct and intuition to make decisions.

God give me the grace not to judge myself or beat myself up about what I am not.

God give me the grace to love myself just as I am.

I read it again and am amused at the repetition of the words 'God give me the grace…' I'd unconsciously chosen these words. I've always preferred to use Higher Power as the alternative to God, but somehow it doesn't work in this prayer. Significant? Not really, I decide.

Our New Home

Friday 8 October

Aix

"Friends are the most important ingredient in this recipe of life." – *Dior Yamasaki*

Today is a day for nurturing friendships, new and old. I muse in my pages about it.

I have many wonderful girlfriends and a few male ones. I'm good at making friends. I think it's because I'm willing to show my vulnerabilities and imperfections. It opens people up and engenders trust. One thing I know for sure is that every person on this planet has a story to tell and that stories connect us.

Everyone has suffered from something at some stage in their life – depression, alcoholism, loneliness, workaholism, food addiction, creative starvation, drug addiction, sex addiction, health problems, family death, physical or mental abuse, perfectionism, hunger, poverty, divorce, financial burdens.

All pain waxes and wanes and so does all pleasure. Our goal in life is to look back and think, I had more joyful days and moments than painful ones, and my life was meaningful and wholehearted.

I list the names of all my friends and family members and think about the pain each one may be suffering. After I write their name, I do a little meditation for them and send them a wish for healing.

Two hours on Skype with two old girlfriends in Australia is enough for me to feel connected again. We share our deepest feelings. We get angry about stuff. We laugh about stuff. We tell each other how much we miss each other and of course I get the obligatory question about whether there are any cute Frenchmen lurking around.

Then I connect over lunch with Florence, the lovely woman I'd met at the school cocktail party. I share my story. She shares hers. By the time lunch is over we share a friendship.

In the evening, Billy and I get together with the gang from French school and their children. We share stories too – funny ones that make us all laugh and complement the pizza and red wine perfectly.

⚜ ⚜ ⚜

Saturday 9 October
Aix

"You can't be at the pole and the equator at the same time. You must choose your own line, as I hope to do, and it is probably colour." – *Vincent van Gogh*

Our New Home

Seeing. Doing. Living. Being. We've been doing lots of living and being here in Provence, but we've barely seen a thing this beautiful country has to offer. So today on this bright brilliant sunshiny Provence day, Richie and his cute twins, Jade and Inés, take us on a trip to the lovely Luberon. Richie is giving us French lessons on the way to visiting Le Domaine de Fotenille and the little village of Lourmarin. He's very patient with me as I ask "Comment dit… (how do you say) sky, flowers, trees?"

The colours of the Luberon are a sight to behold. There's a sky of cornflower blue, clouds of bright white, vine leaves not quite red, not quite pink, but of nature's own unclassifiable colour, pussy willows of café crème, trees of antique olive green, grasses of just plain green, flowers of buttercup yellow, furious pink and ruby red, buildings of sand and caramel, and the rich red earth. My camera loves it. Everything seems so bright and brilliant.

It's been a long time since I've revelled in such colour. I can only imagine how exhilarated and inspired the famous artists of France must have been by nature's palette laid out before them in all its wondrous glory.

Sunday 10 October

Aix

> "My little old dog; A heart-beat at my feet."
> – *Edith Wharton*

Every dog we see brings up sad memories of Dash. It doesn't matter what colour, shape, size or breed. Yet we know Dash is happy with Maureen and Mick, as I regularly email them to find out about his latest escapades.

As we Skype them today it's strange seeing Dash on the screen. He appears to recognise our voices and he seems to know it's us. I can't help but wonder if it's the right thing to keep connected to Dash. Is it fair to confuse him? Has he healed from our abandonment of him?

As we hang up, an incredible sadness comes over us both and we have a little cry and a hug.

Billy spends time with his friends while I write for the rest of the day. It soothes the pain.

Our New Home

Monday 11 October

Aix

"No, there's nothing half so sweet in life as love's young dream." – *Thomas Moore*

I'm living in a state of love. I live without fear, I write in my morning pages. The words are in reference to my financial situation. They come from my heart, not my head. In Sydney I lived in a state of anxiety, particularly around money. I felt trapped by my mortgage and all the other expenses required to live a complicated western lifestyle.

Here in Aix, I have a simple life. I own nothing and I owe nothing. I have no financial fears. I have freedom. I write about my commitment to a simple life when we return to Melbourne; a small apartment, a healthy income and only good debt.

Today I run with purpose. It's short and sharp. I just want to get home and write. And that's what I do until Billy comes home from school full of beans with a beaming smile on his handsome young face.

"What's happening mate?" I ask.

"I have a girlfriend at school. She's from Belgium and she's really hot," he says.

I laugh and ask, "But what's she like on the inside, isn't that what counts?"

"I don't know yet, Mum. I'll let you know when I find out," he quips.

⚜ ⚜ ⚜

Tuesday 12 October

Aix

"The water is your friend… you don't have to fight with water, just share the same spirit as the water, and it will help you move." – Alexandr Popov

At the age of 32 I started swimming, out of necessity, not interest. I had a debilitating back problem that rendered me useless, unable to move, shower myself or go to the toilet unaided.

It scared the hell out of me and my only long-term remedy, according to the physio, was swimming. So I taught myself to swim and I healed my back. And I've swum ever since, not as regularly as I should, but I always come back to it. This great adversity was also my greatest gift. Nine years later I was able to muster up the courage to tackle my fear of the ocean and become a surf lifesaver.

Our New Home

And now as I attempt to swim at Yves Blanc Piscine (pool) in my Coogee surf club swimmers and get into the rhythm, I'm totally distracted. Twenty gorgeous young, buffed rugby types are practising their life-saving skills on a dummy in the lane beside me.

If I'd had the words and the wit, I would've offered to be their real-life dummy and demonstrate the Australian surf life-saving resuscitation technique. I discover with a couple of questions they're bodyguards in training. Shame the bodyguards in Australia don't look like these guys or I'd go clubbing more.

On the way home I drop in to Book in Bar for my book, coffee and music fix. I love the music they play here. Today it's Feist.

An hour later I'm home downloading her on iTunes and discovering more about her. She's a young Canadian singer-songwriter and member of indie rock group Broken Social Scene.

She's a 'feist for the ears' and the inspiration I need to write like a demon for the rest of the day.

⚜ ⚜ ⚜

Wednesday 13 October
Aix

"What you do is infinitely more important than how you do it." – Timothy Ferriss

I've been thinking a lot about my future livelihood lately. I'm keen to create a more organic, creative 'portfolio livelihood' that will allow me to travel, write, speak and make a difference somehow. Loose parameters, I know, but it's all I have to work with right now.

I've been doing some research on organisations that empower women in the not-for-profit sector. Today I Skype with Renata in New York, an amazing woman who co-founded Fitted for Work in Melbourne, a charity that provides work-appropriate clothes for disadvantaged women going for job interviews. She gives me her view on the NFP landscape and the types of organisations I might consider.

Minutes later, I'm out on my artist's date with myself taking photos of flowers in the park surrounding Museum Pavillon Vendôme. That's when I meet Max. He's a dapper older guy with flowing white hair and an impeccably trimmed goatie. He's dressed in a striped shirt, white jeans and clogs, and is scribbling away in his journal while soaking up the sun.

He invites me to sit beside him. It takes less than five minutes of pleasantries before we're chatting about all manner of personal things. He's a gentle, thoughtful and kind man. It's strange that we humans can be so intimate with complete strangers yet lack intimacy with the very ones we love the most.

It turns out that Max is a professor at IAE, Graduate School of Management. By the time I leave he's given me the name and contact details of the person at the school to call about the possibility of me lecturing there. I'm not sure how, or if, it fits into my future plans, but I'm willing to follow all paths that open up to me.

Our New Home

Eventually I bid farewell and continue my meandering journey around the park reflecting on life's small pleasures. Meeting Max was definitely one of those beautiful synchronous experiences. Funny, these experiences seem to be happening more and more as I relax into this most beautiful new life I'm living.

Thursday 14 October
Aix

"Action and reaction, ebb and flow, trial and error, change – this is the rhythm of living. Out of our overconfidence, fear; out of our fear, clearer vision, fresh hope. And out of hope, progress."
– *Bruce Barton*

Today I write from sun up to sun down. Glorious progress. Nothing else to report.

Friday 15 October

Aix

"Raising teenagers is like trying to nail Jell-o to a tree." – Unknown

"I must be totally stark raving mad," I say to Helen over a moules et frite (mussels and French fries) lunch accompanied by a crisp white wine.

Helen is the mother of Owen, one of Billy's friends at school.

"Yes, you are," she says with a laugh. "What were you thinking?"

"That's just it," I admit. "I wasn't thinking. I'm going to need at least a bottle of wine a night to cope."

This weekend Billy and I are playing host to five boys for not one, not two but three nights! We'll have six teenage boys sleeping in our tiny apartment.

I've borrowed mattresses and sleeping bags from Chiara and Claudio, planned the menu and spent all week stocking the fridge to almost overflowing. I've never met these kids before, so I have no idea what I'm in for.

After lunch I head to Book in Bar to meet François, the very brave man who had responded to my very bad singles ad. I'm nervously pacing around the bookshelves wondering why the hell I hadn't thought twice about putting myself out there like

Our New Home

this. Why couldn't I just be happy romancing myself during this time in France?

A man walks in. He looks rather pleasant and I'm hoping it's him but he walks past me and up the stairs. There are only women in the bookshop now, so I'm beginning to wonder if he's stood me up.

Then I hear the rather pleasant man descend the stairs and in a soft half-French and half-English introduction ask, "Excusez-moi. Are you Carolyn?"

"Oui. Je suis Carolyn. Enchanté."

We shake hands and sit down, scrutinising each other and conversing in an odd mix of Frenglish. We're getting on famously, until he tells me he's married. Shit. Now I'm kicking myself for not putting 'célibataire' (single) on the damn ad too. Maybe he's looking for an affair or maybe he really is just interested in improving his English. Maybe I should have been bolder and mentioned I was looking for something more than conversation. Whatever, it's a nice way to spend a couple of hours with this gorgeous French man and get in some practice on how to converse and flirt again.

Our bright burnt orange couch is littered with six handsome, mellow teenage boys attached to various electronic gadgets when I arrive home. I greet them all and leave them to it.

As I sip a glass of red and prepare a huge Mexican meal for them all, I'm silent and present, revelling in the sound of their laughter, jokes, loud music and sudden bursts of rap dancing and singing.

I say nothing. It's a privilege to be a part of this inner sanctum of teenage-hood and a joy to see my son and his friends so happy and free-spirited.

Saturday 16 October

Aix

> "Maybe our girlfriends are our soul mates and guys are just people to have fun with."
> – *Candace Bushnell*

The events of yesterday fuel my thoughts and writing this morning. The boys are still all fast asleep. I write about the joy of having these bright happy beings from various corners of the world in our home, although I wonder if I'll be feeling the same way by Monday morning.

Then my scribblings turn to another topic – François.

He was really quite sexy and we had a lovely flirty time together. He's on his second marriage and has three young children. I wonder if he's looking for an affair?

Affairs appear to be commonplace here. French presidents are just as famous for affairs of the heart as they are for affairs of the country and have set a perfect example for the men and women of this love-addicted country.

But would I have an affair with a married man? It has nothing to do with him or taking the moral high ground. It's all about what is right for me, in my life, right now. I'm still healing and enjoying this time without a man occupying my mind. I don't want to start something with any man who's not truly available to me. I've done that too many times before. I will not initiate further contact with him. If he contacts me, I'll deal with it.

I'm now up and Carolyn's Kitchen is open to feed six hungry boys with breakfast – orange juice, cereal, toast, bacon, eggs and hot chocolate.

Two hours later I've cleaned up and have my shopping list in hand to restock the fridge while the boys head out to the movies. I can see cooking and feeding are going to take precedence over writing this weekend, but I don't mind. My son is really, really happy and that's all that really matters.

Sunday 17 October

Aix

"In quiet places, reason abounds."
– Adlai E Stevenson

The boys are lined up on the couch with computers on laps and iPods in ears, chatting, laughing and singing. The noise is deafening and I'm amazed I can write at all. They leave to go bowling and now the silence is deafening. It takes a full 15 minutes to adjust to it then I write at twice the pace. Bliss.

Monday 18 October
Aix

> "The attention to final form ignores the fact that creativity lies not in the done, but in doing."
> – *Julia Cameron*

I blurt in my journal this morning.

It's very daunting to think that my intimate personal life might be in print and on bookshelves one day. There are lots of books out there like this, though. It's hardly original. Maybe it's just a pipe dream and my writing is total crap.

I stop and take a deep breath and write on some of the antidotes to these negative blurts.

It's not my job to judge my work, to worry about the outcome or be a perfectionist. It's my job, for now, to just do the work, to focus on the quantity, not the quality. I will hand over my fears to my Higher Power. Let her deal with them.

I reluctantly peel myself out of bed to wake all the sleeping bodies for showers to get ready for school. I've served something like 48 meals to six boys over three days. I'm ready to close Carolyn's Kitchen and dine out for the rest of the week.

At last the door closes behind them and I stand alone, surveying the apartment. It looks like a bomb has hit it. I simply can't face it, so I go back to bed.

Our New Home

It takes a full 15 minutes before guilt takes over and I reluctantly get up to tackle the mess. In less than three hours the place is cleaned, mopped and fumigated from top to bottom. As I finish my handy work with a liberal spray of vanilla air freshener, I think how wonderful it is to have a small cosy apartment instead of a big house to clean.

I write the whole afternoon with no distractions and not a single care in the world.

⚜ ⚜ ⚜

Tuesday 19 October
Aix

"Business opportunities are like buses, there's always another one coming." – Richard Branson

Billy leaves for school still in a bit of a coma from the weekend's festivities. The door closes behind him and 10 minutes later I'm on Skype with Jane, the CEO of Fitted for Work.

I find out more about her and the wonderful work they do. She finds out more about me. We establish a connection. There may be the potential for work when I return to Melbourne, or there may not. It's not something I'm attached to as I take the first steps to creating a new livelihood. I'm just grateful my CV looks pretty good after all these years of being in business and that I have the networks and contacts to help make my vision a reality.

After a blissful yoga lesson I have a healthy vegetarian lunch with Lucia, Elizabeth and Andrew at Toute une Histoire. And of course the afternoon is filled with my favourite pastime, writing.

⚜ ⚜ ⚜

Wednesday 20 October
Aix

"Goals are the fuel in the furnace of achievement."
– Brian Tracy

There are only two simple goals for today – to go on my artist's date with myself and write.

I take my camera out for another photography session and take shots of restaurant signs, moss-covered buildings, washing hanging from windows, fountains and statues.

There's one statue on the corner of a building that particularly piques my interest. It's a statue of Mary dressed in

Our New Home

rose pink robes with a plump baby Jesus balanced on her hip. She gazes towards the sky with a serene face full of sadness, resignation and detachment. She doesn't look lovingly into her child's eyes or bear even a hint of a smile. Maybe it's because she knows full well that her son is not hers alone and that one day he'll be persecuted and nailed to the cross.

That gets me thinking about all the paintings and statues I've seen of Mary and Jesus throughout my life. In every one there's been total disconnection between mother and son. Sad.

I reluctantly end my photography jaunt and sit down for a café crème and a salad niçoise at my local before heading home to write for the rest of the day. I achieve my two simple daily goals with ease and grace and I'm blissfully content.

Thursday 21 October
Aix

"The secret of your future is hidden in your daily routine." – Mike Murdock

I'm annoyed with Billy this morning. It feels like I have to nag him from sun up to sun down. Billy, get up. Billy, have a shower. Billy, get dressed. Billy, eat your breakfast. Billy, pack your school bag. Billy, do your teeth. Billy, go now or you'll miss the bus. Billy, get off your computer and do your homework.

It's like he's dependent on me as his body clock. At times I feel like it's taking its toll on me, and him.

This morning he's being particularly bad at getting organised, and extra surly with me, and I'm particularly short with him. I don't like myself when I get like this. Is it just me or does every parent of a teenager feel like this at times?

My morning pages are filled with rants about it before I segue to a list of ideas that I could adopt to make it easier on us both. When I finish, I'm settled and a little happier. I send Grace an email to organise a Skype session to come up with some strategies on how to deal with it. I don't have to handle this on my own. It's okay to ask for help.

I pull on my well-worn running gear to meet Elizabeth. It's wonderful having her as my running companion to huff and puff with. We chatter lots while we run a couple of laps of Parc de la Torse before I rush home. I've never been so eager to get to work in my entire life.

I write for the rest of the day. The routine is really starting to kick in and I'm truly starting to see some results.

Our New Home

Friday 22 October

Aix

> "Discipline is the bridge between goals and accomplishment." – *Jim Rohn*

There's a synchronised swimming team at the pool this morning. While not quite as appealing as the bodyguards, I'm in awe of the young women's fitness and grace. Yet somehow it's their discipline that's most impressive. They execute the same move over and over again to a point of exquisite perfection. They have a single-minded goal and they're 100 per cent disciplined.

As I watch them, mesmerised, I reflect on that word – 'discipline'. In the past 10 years I've rebelled against it. It's been something to avoid at all costs, a negative concept opposed to my personal ideal of liberalism, creativity and freedom. Yet it's a beautiful, productive, helpful word too.

I realise I can be creative and disciplined. I can be spontaneous and disciplined. I can live on the other side of the world and still be disciplined. I can write and be disciplined. I decide I like the word and I want more of it.

After my lesson in self-discipline, I shower and dress semi-professionally for a meeting with the IAE, Graduate School of Management in Puyricard, about 15 minutes from Aix.

I'm keen to make as many connections as possible while here in order to open up future work opportunities. I'd followed up the introduction from Max and received a warm invitation for a meeting with Vèronique at the school.

By the time I leave, I have an invitation to come back next year to speak at their International Business seminars. While I'm not sure if I'll be able to make it, I'm excited that it's even a possibility.

Billy is on holidays for two weeks from today. He comes home happy to consume his after-school snacks – baguette, some grapes and a chocolat éclair – before dinner at Elizabeth and Andrew's, our Canadian friends.

Lapin (rabbit) wrapped in bacon and lemon and thyme atop a tomato purée and fettuccine is on the menu. It's our first taste of rabbit here in France and we love it.

Andrew and Elizabeth are on a three-month holiday in Aix to be followed by a trek up Mount Kilimanjaro and then a long stint in Melbourne. The synchronicity of this doesn't escape us. By the time we leave, I know this wonderful couple will be friends for a lifetime. Sometimes one just knows these things.

Our New Home

Saturday 23 October

Aix

"I do yoga so I can stay flexible enough to kick my own arse if necessary." – Betsy Canas Garmon

He's back again. And I'm pissed off. I dreamt about him last night… I write in my morning pages.

I know it's because I'm reliving the events for the book. Is this writing healing me or hurting me?

I finish my three pages with a smile and a final statement.

Get up sleepy head. Embrace the day!

So I do. Billy and I snuggle up over a hot chocolate and talk about the plans for our holidays and our train trip to Italy before I head off to yoga.

This morning's practice is accompanied by live music. The sun salutations energise me and warm me up inside and out, as I concentrate on the gentle rhythm of the drums and sit-guitar to lead me deep into my practice.

By the time I leave I'm in a state of bliss and ready for my artist's date with myself. This time it's a date with a difference – a meditation and prayer in Cathédrale Saint Sauveur.

I enter the cathedral in silence, focusing on my steady breath and my beautiful surroundings. I take in every holy painting, every imperfect wooden beam, every magnificent stained-glass window, every stiff-backed pew, every little red-carpeted prayer stool, every flickering candle and the ostentatious marble pulpit.

I discover an uninhabited alcove with its own private altar and sit down on the hard pew, eyes closed, face cast forward and heart open. I start with my artist's prayer then ask my Higher Power, 'What shall I pray for today?'

'Love,' she answers.

So I pray for love in that cathedral. Not just for a man's love, but for more self-love and to be more loving towards others. I pray for love for my son, for my family, for my friends, for all the people who have graced my life and all those who never will. I pray gently, not hard. I pray with faith, not desperation. I pray with hope, not expectation. I have no idea how long I pray for love, but the gurgling of my stomach brings me abruptly out of prayer, reminding me that I've not eaten today. It sends me straight to the boulangerie.

Tonight Billy and I are attending *Empty Moves* at Pavillon Noir, a contemporary ballet by the famous French choreographer and dancer Angelin Preljocaj.

The curtain rises and the audience leans forward in anticipation as four beautiful young dancers enter the stage in their bright mismatched underwear. The dance moves change from wild abandonment to focused constraint and back to wild abandonment again.

There's no music bringing them to these highs and lows, just an interesting cacophony of sounds and a monotonous voice-over that somehow seems totally out of place.

I'm intrigued by this ballet, but not enamoured of it. And as for Billy, he falls asleep on my shoulder within five minutes of it starting and jumps to attention right at the end when everyone is clapping.

"They're only clapping because it's over," he announces. Priceless.

Sunday 24 October
Aix

"Fat gives things flavor." – Julia Child

Billy is still fast asleep as I go out for my morning run with Elizabeth. I'm getting better at this running thing. I can now run about 8 kilometres with only a couple of stops for a short stretch. It feels fabulous to be getting so fit again.

We're now at brunch with Chiara and Claudio in Café Madeleine. In Australia brunch is a big deal and a weekend ritual – crispy bacon, scrambled, fried or poached eggs, sauces and condiments of every kind from tomato to pesto and hollandaise, roasted tomatoes, avocado, fried mushrooms, baked beans, sausages, corn fritters with tomato relish and breads of every variety. It's pretty much a real fat-fest and an essential cure for the hangover most Aussies are so good at acquiring.

Here in France, not eating before 1pm is de rigueur. A tiny corner of a croissant taken with un café is all that's required to sustain the French until the real eating starts at le dèjeuner with the plat du jour (today's special).

I'm starving after a run and Billy is a 182-cm tall teenage boy, so the corner of a croissant at 11am just won't cut it. We order the eggs and bacon and eat with gusto while everyone around us nibbles delicately on their pastry.

Monday 25 October

Aix

"Our intention creates our reality." – *Wayne Dyer*

While I'm focusing every day on the creative process of writing and trying not to be attached to the outcome, I'm still writing with intent. And the intent is that one day this book will be published. So today I'm taking my first tiny brave step in that direction. I search the internet and look for a book publishing proposal document and subscribe to a few self-publishing websites. It's only a few gentle steps but it feels good.

Billy rests. I write. We're both happy.

Our New Home

Tuesday 26 October

Aix

"The world is a book and those who do not travel, read only a page." – Saint Augustine

Tomorrow we're off to Italy! Our plan is to take the train from Aix to Venice over 10 days with stop-offs in Monaco, Genova, Florence and Venice. I've booked only the train and hotel in Monaco and the return flight from Venice to Marseille. The rest in between will be organised on the fly.

So much for Bernie's 7 Ps, I think to myself as we pack our bags and clean up the apartment.

There's only one thing left to do before we go and that's get Billy a haircut. Downstairs we go to the funky coiffure, Sculpt, right next door. We walk in. Every guy has tattoos, wild hair, big holes in their ears and jeans that somehow stay up despite sitting way below their bum cheeks.

After some loose instructions in Frenglish, I leave them to it for a spot of shopping. Thirty minutes later I come back to Billy, who is surly and unhappy but with a great haircut.

"It looks fantastic," I say, truly meaning it.

"I look like Justin Bieber," he mumbles. "I hate it. Can I have the keys? I'm going home to wash it out."

As I hand him the keys, I decide there's simply no point in reasoning with him.

We have a pleasant, uneventful dinner and an early night. I can hear Billy gently snoring in the loft above me, while the soft light of my bedside lamp illuminates my computer and I write.

There's a nice hot chocolate on my bedside table sitting amongst my books and journals. Cosy and content is how I feel.

4
Our Italian Adventure

France to Italy

Wednesday 27 October
Aix to Monaco, France

> "Fear those not who argue, but those who dodge."
> – Marie Ebner-Eschenbach

My morning pages are filled with concern.

I'm a bit worried about this trip with Billy. He's more interested in socialising and having fun with his friends than exploring Italy with me. We've settled into a good routine here and now I'm upsetting it with 10 days of relentless train travel, hotels and sightseeing. We'll be together 24/7. Are we going to survive it?

I'm fearful that we'll have a miserable time and annoyed that he's not more interested in exploring France and Italy with me. I rant some more and finally remember the wise words from Grace: "Maybe this time in France is not about having the great travelling adventure. Maybe it's a time for peace and rest and healing for you and Billy."

After an uneventful train trip from Aix to Marseille through Nice we arrive at the hotel in Monaco, a tiny country on the Mediterranean Sea. After we unpack and go for a walk, my worst fears are realised. Billy just doesn't want to be here and is now extremely angry. He yells at me for no apparent reason and without any explanation turns on his heel and walks back in the direction of the hotel.

At first I'm angry, but then extreme sadness sets in and tears overwhelm me. Eventually I calm down enough to follow him back to the hotel and let him into the room.

"Order what you want from the in-room menu. I'll be back in a few hours," I tell him, tight-lipped.

I go sadly in search of a place that will remind me of home and give me some comfort. I happen upon a totally empty but comforting Old English pub, buy a packet of cigarettes (my occasional unhealthy default habit when I'm in pain) and a Fosters beer and write furiously in my journal.

I write about my failings as a mother and all the things I could've done to handle this experience differently. After six cigarettes and three Fosters I've calmed down enough to be writing legibly and rationally, despite the beer. After a few pages I come to the blinding realisation that a nice run would've been a far better option for vanquishing my anger than sitting in a pub.

Finally I let myself back into the hotel room to face Billy.

"Sorry, son, I didn't handle that whole experience very well. Please forgive me."

And Billy says, "Sorry, Mum, I don't know what got into me."

We both shed a few tears and we talk openly about how we're feeling about this whole experience – not just in Italy but the whole time in France.

We hug for a long time before sleep takes over.

Thursday 28 October
Monaco to Genova, Italy

"Have a deep respect for the source of life and also for the ocean, for the forest, for the stars and for the truth."
– Unknown

After yesterday's spectacular performance we now only have a morning to see the whole country of Monaco before we take the train to Italy. It's just lucky that it's the second smallest country in the world (after The Vatican, that is).

We walk along the harbour looking at the incredibly ostentatious super yachts in this tax-free billionaires' playground. We take the tourist train around this country the size of New York's Central Park and home to just 35,000 people.

We discover a bit about the Grimaldi family who've ruled Monaco since 1297. The romance and tragedy surrounding Prince Rainier, Princess Grace (Grace Kelly) and their three headstrong children, Caroline, Albert and Stephanie, is palpable and fills every corner of this beautiful tiny country. Home to the famous Monte-Carlo Grand-Prix, the Monte-Carlo Casino and numerous James Bond movies, it's easy to see why Monaco draws crowds from all over the world.

We have enough time to visit the fabulous Musée Océanographique, perched precariously on the cliffs of Monaco. It's the most beautiful aquarium we've been to, after Sydney's of course. It's cloaked in darkness and silence and the tanks are full of fish, at peace with their lot in life. For a brief moment, I envy these fish, with no storms to endure, predators to hide from or livelihood to forage for.

Eighty euros later we arrive by taxi in Ventimiglia, Italy, after being told the trains are not running due to a strike. We have 30 minutes to kill before the train to Genova arrives so we stop for our first-ever Italian gelati on Italian soil.

After one lick Billy announces, "I absolutely love Italy!"

I'm amused at how drastically things can change in just 24 hours, all thanks to a simple ice cream, but of course don't say a word.

While the Italian trains appear to be a bit grubbier than the trains of their French neighbours, at least they're not on strike and are on schedule. We make it to Genova in no time at all and dump our bags to rush out for our very first Italian pizza. Food, glorious Italian food!

⚜ ⚜ ⚜

Friday 29 October
Genova, Italy

"Against you I will fling myself, unvanquished and unyielding. O death!" – *Virginia Wolfe*

The morning pages are no more positive than yesterday.

I'm still unsettled about the situation between Billy and I. He really doesn't seem to want to be on this journey. I'm trying to jolly him along and give him down time, but he still doesn't seem interested. To be honest, I wish I could send him back on the first plane home. Is that a shocking thing for a mother to write?

It's a cathartic experience being able to write about this. It's better for me to vent on the pages, than vent at my son.

Genova is an important seaport in the Ligurian region and has both an urbane and medieval feel to it. It's the gateway to the famous Cinque Terre, the home of pesto sauce and Christopher Columbus, and the word 'jeans' was derived from its name.

The day's events include a bus tour around the city, a trip to yet another aquarium to see the enormous and gorgeous dugongs, and a walk around the port and the magnificent Piazza de Ferrari and the surrounding streets.

It's late afternoon when I drop Billy back to the hotel, grab my camera and catch a taxi to the famous Cimitero monumentale di Staglieno. The sun is starting to set as I enter the front gates of the world's most awe-inspiring cemetery. I walk around slowly, in a meditative state breathing deeply and taking in every tiny detail.

I stop to spend some time in the children's cemetery with its small well-tended plots adorned with sculptures of cherubs and crosses and family portraits. There's a youngish couple tending a plot. I can't imagine how unbearable it must be for them, to have lost a child, and how painful it must be to come back month after month, year after year.

I climb up into the hilly recesses of the cemetery and photograph the family crypts – mini churches complete with spire and bell, and wonder how many mothers, fathers, brothers, sisters, husbands, wives and children must be buried there.

I walk past the rows and rows of small square boxes bearing the ashes, photos and plaques of loved ones more recently deceased. Then I move on to the big, arched halls that house magnificently intricate statues and storyboards depicting the lives of the people laid to rest beneath, including Oscar Wilde's wife, Constance Lloyd.

There's one statue that really haunts me. It's of a young girl. Her eyes are cast downwards over a cross she's holding close to her chest. The hooded cloak she wears casts a dark shadow over her eyes. There's an immense sadness and resignation in those eyes that no child should ever have to bear. Yet her face and lips are soft and childlike, untainted. I photograph her from every angle and gaze upon her face until a few tears start to moisten the corners of my eyes.

On my return to the front gates, I pass a building with maybe a dozen coffins inside awaiting designation to their final resting place as the last of the day's mourners take their leave.

I've been to many cemeteries in my lifetime, but none so heart-rendingly sad and haunting as Staglieno.

After this mournful experience, I'm in need of a little cheering up, so Billy and I have aperitifs in our lovely hotel cocktail bar before heading out to dinner at Genio's – a Genoan institution. We consume with gusto a very traditional meal of pesto spaghetti, antipasto, artichoke ravioli and veal bits in garlic and olive oil. The food is inexpensive, fresh, simple and exquisitely delicious.

Saturday 30 October

Genova to Riomaggiore, Italy

> "In order to keep a true perspective of one's importance, everyone should have a dog that will worship him and a cat that will ignore him."
> – *Unknown*

After the last few days I opt for quick, positive morning pages. I end them with *Get your head out of your butt and get into life*.

I laugh, snap shut my journal and get Billy up so we can fuel up at the hotel buffet before saying "Arrivederci Genova".

The train takes us to Riomaggiore, the most southern village in the chain of five that make up the famous Cinque Terre – Monterosso, Vernazza, Corniglia, Manarola and Riomaggiore. We lug our bags up to our hotel, which is, of course, halfway up a mountain cliff. Luckily we're distracted from our huffing and puffing by the quaint baby pink, warm apricot and pale yellow houses flanking us on both sides. The lovingly tended market gardens and vineyards provide a cool backdrop to the houses, and the ocean cliffs below remain majestic, despite their growing distance. This village is at once rugged and relentless, and peaceful and serene. It takes my breath away, literally.

The path between these five villages is touted to be the most beautiful (and most trekked) in the world and I can totally understand why as we spend the rest of the afternoon hopping between each village by foot and train.

We're now at dinner, ending our superb day in the Cinque Terre at Riomaggiore's La Grotto restaurant. We're greeted by the maitre d', Signore Cat, who escorts us to our table and promptly jumps into Billy's lap to become our sleek and purring dinner companion. He has a white chest, white-tipped paws and deep green eyes.

He looks at Billy, as if to say, "What are you waiting for? I'm hungry. Feed me!"

We're amazed that the staff just laugh and cluck at Signore Cat instead of shooing him out. But if they don't mind, we don't mind. He's truly lovely.

As we're served olives, antipasto, frittata, pesto, and potato pasta with stuffed breaded pesto mussels, Signore Cat isn't disappointed until a gentle nip to Billy's hand, obviously for not feeding him enough, causes him to hastily remove him from his lap.

Signore Cat is not miffed in the slightest as he sticks his tail in the air and without even a second glance prowls off to another table to try his luck.

Funny but true and only in Italy!

Sunday 31 October

Riomaggiore to Florence, Italy

"The thing women have yet to learn is that nobody gives you power. You just take it." – Roseanne Barr

My morning pages are filled with random musings that have come from my deep sub-conscious. They're all about why I'm writing this book and what I hope to achieve from publishing it.

Life, for many women, is messy, lonely and sometimes really, really shitty. I'm writing this book to heal myself and help other women feel empowered to overcome whatever problems in life they may be facing so they can live their life with purpose and passion. I want women to feel empowered to change whatever is not serving them, to live with authenticity and creativity, to make a better life for themselves and their children and to make a difference to other women. This book is a tribute to women everywhere.

I write for many more pages about the love and compassion I feel for all women and their potential to heal the world. When I simply have no more words in me, I close my journal and pray silently for us all.

The train takes us from Riomaggiore to La Spezia, Pisa, and then the heart of Tuscany – Firenze (Florence). It's all smooth 'training' and not for the first time I'm grateful I'd decided not to drive.

Our Italian Adventure

It's wet and dreary and not the best day for sight-seeing as I guide Billy along the streets of Firenze, aware that at any moment the Duomo, The Basilica di Santa Maria del Fiore, is going to make its presence felt. We turn the corner and Billy exclaims, "Oh my God, Mum, look!"

There it is. I knew it would be breathtaking but I simply wasn't prepared for how overwhelmingly awe-inspiring it is. It takes one second, despite the rain, to fall in love with Firenze.

We stroll around the Duomo, taking it in from every angle while deftly trying to avoid having our eyes poked out by the umbrellas of other awestruck tourists. The 414 steps of the tower to view the Piazza del Duomo, the Baptistry and Giotto's Campanile does not disappoint.

The interior is rather gothic, empty and barren and quite the contrast to the Notre Dame. I wonder how austere the lives of its inhabitants must have been. I'm still ambivalent about all these monuments to God, however I fully appreciate their beauty and just revel in the experience.

The most famous Firenze institution, Gilli's, beckons us for a snack while we gaze over the Piazza. The gilded glass mirrors, chandeliers, panelled walls and stained-glass windows make a perfect setting for the chocolates, marzipan fruits and cakes that look far too exquisite for human consumption. We walk out with our stomachs a little heavier, my wallet much lighter and in mellow, happy spirits.

It's pizza again for dinner, just for something different, and at an unremarkable but cheap and cheerful restaurant. It's rustic and cosy and we're both happy.

Before I turn out the light, for some reason my fingers start to itch and I feel compelled to study them at length. They've served me well, these fingers, these tools of my trade. I've chosen not to use them while in Italy, for book writing that is. But now I'm feeling an urge to set them flying again. 'Just one more week,' I tell them, as though they can hear me. Weird.

⚜ ⚜ ⚜

Monday 1 November
FLORENCE, ITALY

"Wine is the most civilised thing in the world."
– *Ernest Hemingway*

It's All Saints public holiday, the whole of Florence is shut down and, to top it off, it's still wet and drizzly. Never to be defeated, I head down to the concierge to find something we can do.

Two hours later, much to Billy's annoyance, we're lining up for a bus tour to the Chianti region.

Even on this overcast day, the muted autumn colours blend together in unrivalled beauty and serenity. The region is littered with hundreds of old castles that once belonged to farmers when Chianti wine was all about quantity, not quality. About 30 or so years ago the farmers sold up their castles for a song to expats. Now with fewer and better producers, the quality of the Chianti wine is superb and buying a castle to make your home is next to impossible.

At Castello Il Palagio winery we're treated to four classic wines starting with a rosé, followed by a Chianti Classico, a Super Red and a dessert wine.

And the accompanying food? Bread rubbed with garlic, lightly toasted and dripping with extra virgin olive oil with less than 1 per cent acidity, and biscotti to dip in the dessert wine before sucking and crunching. Yum.

On the meandering route towards home we stop off at a popular tourist village, Greve, to discover Antica Macerelleria Falorni, a shop filled with meats and cheeses from all over Italy.

It's almost a sensory overload. Cured meats hang from every corner and the smell down in the cheese cellar is overwhelmingly pungent. It's the highlight of Billy's day as we taste test our way around the shop and make some significant purchases, including a nice slab of wild boar salami. Saporito!

As we take our leave and the bus trawls slowly homeward, I ponder the idea of an extended vacation in Firenze and the Chianti region in the not too distant future. No harm in dreaming!

Tuesday 2 November

FLORENCE, ITALY

> "Therefore, let there be two Venuses in the soul, the one heavenly, the other earthly. Let them both have a love, the Heavenly for the reflection upon divine beauty, the earthly for generating divine beauty in earthly." – *From Ficino's Commentary on Plato's Symposium*

Fat feelings get the better of me this morning and are the subject of my morning pages.

I don't really like my body at all today. We've been on the road six days now and I haven't done one lick of exercise, other than walking around and bending my elbows to eat and drink. I'm beginning to feel sluggish and fat.

I've sometimes struggled with my weight although I'm fortunate that genetics blessed me with height and long, lean limbs so I can bear a couple of extra kilograms until I wise up and work it off.

I'm not always so diligent about watching what I put in my mouth and my boobs and stomach seem to be the first to appreciate any increased dietary intake. As I've got older and wiser however, I've become more accepting of my body and appreciative of all its beautiful flaws and imperfections.

I end the pages with… Who cares? Enjoy it while I can. When I get home after my birthday, I'll get back into my healthy eating and exercise regimen.

Our Italian Adventure

It's a beautiful, sunny day in Florence today as we stroll to the Accademia di Belle Arti Di Firenze to see Michelangelo's statue of David. Michelangelo was of course a genius of the Renaissance Period along with da Vinci. He was also a painter (the Sistine Chapel and The Last Judgment), an architect, engineer, mathematician, philosopher and poet, who happened to also study anatomy and physiology intently enough to be able to sculpt the perfect body.

Legend has it that he and da Vinci used to conduct covert autopsies on the bodies of deceased homeless people so they could study the human body first-hand. This was a time when the church ruled the existence, and thinking, of all people. Together with a handful of other influential intellects and dilettantes, these amazing men brought about the Renaissance period, which paved the way for the free-thinking, intellectual world we now live in.

David is simply incredible. At 5.17 metres, this biblical hero was sculpted between 1501 and 1504 by the 25-year-old Michelangelo. His gentle giant-like hands and feet are of totally disproportionate size to his penis, yet his muscular stomach, chest, arms and buttocks are every woman's dream.

Veins bulging, face tense, brow furrowed, there's fear in his eyes as he appears poised to battle Goliath. One can only imagine what he might have been thinking and feeling, were he a real man.

We're now at the Uffizi Gallery, one of the oldest and most famous art museums in the world, to see more of the masters and discover the history of painting from the one-dimensional religious paintings of Mary and her baby to the Renaissance paintings of Botticelli.

My absolute favourite is the Birth of Venus, a painting commissioned by the wealthy, political, banking family of Medici around 1486. It depicts the goddess Venus, pale and voluptuous, emerging on the seashore as a fully-grown woman with her long blonde tresses and hair covering her breasts and pubic area. She's standing in a scallop shell thought to depict the woman's vulva and is being lovingly gazed upon by two wind deities, Zephyr and Chloris, and Hora who conveys time and seasons.

This painting, like its twin La Primerva, painted almost 10 years before, has many interpretations – mythological, spiritual, political and religious. My own interpretation is simple. I see a beautiful, vulnerable and empowered goddess, a woman who is adored in all her glorious nakedness.

The Uffizi is a pure delight, but not as delightful as witnessing the attention Billy is paying to our brilliant storytelling guide and the way he's scrutinising each work of art she's showing us. Our guide has humanised the scenes depicted in the paintings and given us a real insight into the lives of the artists behind them. She has Billy (and me) hooked.

On the way home we chat about all the art we've seen, our favourite paintings and what we've loved about glorious Firenze, and we agree that three days is just simply not enough.

Our Italian Adventure

Wednesday 3 November

Venice, Italy

"Venice is like eating an entire box of chocolate liqueurs in one go." – Truman Capote

Today's morning pages topic? Loneliness.

I feel lonely today for some reason, despite being here with my son. Interesting. I know it's completely possible to feel lonely with a partner. Been there, done that. Loneliness as a single woman is somehow more pure. I don't have to hide it. I can admit it to myself and my girlfriends and we talk about it openly. In a relationship, loneliness can remain hidden and unaddressed until a crisis of some description is subconsciously manifested in order to bring it into the open.

The morning pages are truly the best meditative practice I've ever undertaken. It's now eight weeks since I first started them. When I attempted my first pages, I was embarrassed by the self-centred drivel that erupted from nowhere. Now I don't judge at all and I just blurt. The pages are helping me uncover and acknowledge my deepest feelings, arrive at decisions, be a better mother, rediscover my creative streak and of course write, write, write.

After a two-hour train trip we arrive in Venezia (Venice), the incredible city built on a malarial swamp some time as long ago as the 5th century.

Straight from the train we hop onto a number one ferry that takes us right down the Grand Canale. Is there any more glorious entry into any city in the world, than this entrance into Venice? There are merchant boats loaded with goods and fresh produce, taxi boats, ferries, gondolas, fishing boats on their way out to sea and all manner of ancient and magnificent Gothic palaces, churches and apartment blocks lining the canal.

On first impression Venice is astoundingly glittery, lavish and chic. I can't wait to see what lies beneath.

We're unloaded and drag our cases through the Piazza San Marco where people are standing statue-like with pigeons crawling all over them and scrabbling around for seed being haphazardly strewn around.

A gondola ride, while expensive and a bit touristy, is our first up-close and personal experience of the waterways of Venice and the incredible layering of different eras and architectural styles. We're taken on a journey through the twisted maze of waterways with one of the 400 gondoliers of Venice.

Basilica Di San Marco is our next port of call. Luminous angels set in gold mosaics trumpet us into the church. The marble columns and floors, domes of glass and gold mosaics and alabaster chalices give an overall impression of sheer opulence.

Then we happen upon the Pala d'Oro altarpiece, a hidden treasure boasting over 2000 emeralds, rubies, sapphires and gemstones and depicting lively biblical scenes. I love the Basilica, but as we leave I can't help but think how many starving countries its glorious booty could feed.

Billy is not feeling well tonight so opts to stay in with a pizza while I enjoy dinner at Al Mascaron with Andrew and Elizabeth, who are also visiting Venice from Aix. It's superb to say the least. We're served a seafood appetiser of prawns, sardines, calamari and polenta, followed by mussel, clam and shrimp spaghetti and biscotti dipped in dessert wine and coffee! It's nice to go somewhere authentic that's filled with locals and that doesn't have a 'touristique' menu.

Thursday 4 November
VENICE, ITALY

"A painter paints pictures on canvas. But musicians paint their pictures on silence." – Leopold Stokowski

Today we navigate our way through the streets of Venice to find the ferry that will take us to Murano and Burano, the delightful fishing villages about 45 minutes away.

At Murano we take a stroll in an attempt to see some glass factories at work. Alas it seems there are few and that much of the glassware that Venice is famous for is actually not even produced here anymore. It's a pleasant town but not as aesthetically exquisite and vibrant as Burano.

Unlike the homes of the Cinque Terre, which are painted in soft, muted colours, the homes of Burano are painted in wild and vivid ones: lime green, lemon yellow, orange orange, screaming pink and brilliant blue.

Despite their clashing colours, they're in complete harmony with each other. The houses line the canals, which are filled with tiny bobbing fishing vessels, throughout the village.

Burano must be one of the happiest places on earth, if not for the villagers, at least for budding photographers like us. Even Billy decides to take up the challenge of attempting to take the best and most brilliant photo of our holiday.

We've been told an absolutely must-do experience in Venice is to take an aperitivo in Piazza San Marco. As we drink and feast on succulent olives from the famous Café Florian, a favourite haunt of Dickens, Hemmingway and Casanova, we take in the glorious strains of the orchestra, the skyline over the Basilica and the buildings framing the piazza. The exquisite beauty being bestowed upon us in this moment causes me to wonder what it would have been like to be an artist in Venice, in this very café, in a bygone era.

Friday 5 November
Venice, Italy

"You must be the change you wish to see in the world." – *Mahatma Gandhi*

We're off to see Peggy's collection today. Peggy Guggenheim, that is. I'm as fascinated by her life as I am with her art collection.

Peggy G was well known as a collector of men, not just art. At age 21, she inherited a small fortune years after her father went down with the *Titanic*. She got involved with the bohemian artistic community in Paris so left New York to live in the Montparnasse quarter. Later she opened a gallery and a museum in London, and amassed, over many years, a large collection of abstract, surreal and cubist works of art – Picasso, Dali, Congdon, Pollock and Chagall amongst many others. She established the gallery in Venice after World War II.

There's one piece of art that captivates me. It's a neon-tube-lit sign by Maurizio Nannucci attached to the outside wall in the garden of the home. It says 'Changing Place. Changing Time. Changing Thought. Changing Future.' I stare at it intently and contemplate the words and their relevance to my life, and Billy's.

It's over five months since I radically changed my thoughts, which in turn changed the place we now find ourselves in, and ultimately the course of our future. I'm very keen to give Billy a sense of certainty over his future (at least he has five years of school ahead of him). As for me, all I know is that right now, unlike five months ago, I'm okay with not knowing what the future holds and I have faith it will work out just as it's meant to.

We end our last day in Venice with a pigeon-feeding frenzy in Piazza San Marco followed by our last traditional Italian dinner – bruschetta, cold meats, pasta and gelati.

"No more pasta, pizza or gelati from tomorrow," I say to Billy. My gorgeous 182cm son, who could eat pizza morning, noon and night, barely looks up from his plate and says, "Sure, Mum."

⚜ ⚜ ⚜

Saturday 6 November
Venice to Aix

"Where thou art, that is home." – *Emily Dickinson*

Today we make our way back to Aix by plane. It's a long and uneventful day. Within two minutes of arriving back at the apartment we call home, Billy plonks himself on the couch with his computer. He looks as happy as Larry.

"Who said routine was boring?" he quips.

"Thanks, mate, for coming on this journey with me. We've had our moments but I'm very glad we did it and I love you very much."

"I love you too, Mum," he says without looking up.

5
Back in Aix

Home is Where the Heart is

Sunday 7 November
Aix, My birthday

"There is a fountain of youth: it is your mind, your talents, the creativity you bring to your life and the lives of people you love. When you learn to tap this source, you will truly have defeated age."
– Sophia Loren

Today is my 47th birthday.

I start my morning pages by reflecting on the year that was – the past.

I reflect on how stuck I was and my courage to change. Then, inexplicably, the words flow into a reflection on the future. I start writing a whole string of goals for myself – continue to improve my health and fitness, nurture Billy so that he's happy and settled in Melbourne, find a livelihood that I love, get this book published, find a house and set up a home – and on and on it goes.

I poise mid-sentence and wonder why I've just written about the past and the future. How about what's happening right now, this second?

I breathe deeply and slowly survey my room, taking in every small detail – the lamp on my bedside table with its shade tilting at a jaunty angle, the stack of books and journals piled haphazardly next to it, the dark forest-green walls and my comfy striped bedcover.

I listen to the toll of the church bells, Billy snoring in his bed upstairs in the loft, the sounds of the café owners chatting as they open for business, and the motorbikes whizzing past.

After a long time I return to my journal and fill my third page with gratitude.

I am grateful to be healing and becoming more whole every day. I am grateful for being free, here and now in this room, in this city, in this country, in France. I am grateful for my son and my brand new friends who are going to celebrate my birthday with me today.

Minutes later Billy comes in, jumps on my bed with a birthday card and gift, and sings Happy Birthday. I read the card aloud.

Dear Mum

Thanks for being the best mum ever. I know I've been a massive pain lately. Spending more time with each other is driving us crazy. But thanks so much for sticking through it and being such a lovely, caring and understanding parent. You are truly the greatest mum a boy could ever ask for. I love you so much and always will, unless we kill each other first!

Love from Billy

It's not often that words escape me, but right now I feel so much love for my son and his humorous and insightful words, that I'm rendered speechless.

It's 9am now and I have a dozen or more people coming for brunch in just two hours. What was I thinking lolling around in bed indulging myself on my birthday?

After a quick shower, I head down to the markets to stock up on flowers, breads, petit fours, fruits, wine, terrines, cheeses, tapenade, olives and anything that stirs my interest and palate.

Our newfound friends from all corners of the world arrive. Most of them don't know each other but it doesn't take long before our cosy, inviting artist's retreat is full of conversation and laughter, kids and adults alike. It's a wonderful, happy, connected day.

As I settle down to sleep, I think fondly of all the friends and family who have emailed and Skyped to wish me a happy birthday. But there's no message from James. I'd half thought he'd at least acknowledge my birthday, but nothing. It feels like any connection, love and friendship we shared is completely dead, done and dusted. My happy day ends in a little sadness.

Back in Aix

Monday 8 November
Aix

> "I learned that you should feel when writing, not like Lord Byron on a mountain top, but like a child stringing beads in kindergarten – happy, absorbed and quietly putting one bead on after another."
> – *Brenda Ueland*

Billy bounces out of bed to get back to school this morning. He can't wait to see his friends (and his girlfriend of course).

After my morning pages, I meet Elizabeth for a run. It's great to be back exercising – and chatting – again.

I'm excited as I run up the stairs two at a time to the apartment. It feels like I'm about to be reunited with a long-lost lover. Only it's not a lover, it's my computer.

I don't even stop to take a shower. I sit down at my little red desk, pull out a purple sheet of card, fold it in half and write

My goal: To have completed the first draft of my book by 1.1.11.
Action Plan: September to be finished by 28.11.10; October by 11.12.10; November by 24.12.10; December by 1.1.11.

I decorate my card with sparkles and love hearts, and place it on my desk.

I take a shower, put on Canadian band Arcade Fire, my latest music fetish introduced courtesy of Elizabeth and Andrew and sit down to start work.

It's like the self-enforced break from writing has given me a renewed energy and focus. Words fly into my brain and travel down my neck, shoulders, arms and fingers to the keyboard, where they manifest themselves on the screen right in front of me. There's simply no better feeling than the bliss I feel when I write.

⚜ ⚜ ⚜

Tuesday 9 November
Aix

"In order to recover as an artist, you must be prepared to be a bad artist. Give yourself permission to be a beginner." – Julia Cameron

I'm seriously doubting my writing ability. I need some inspiration. Even after a day of pure flow yesterday, I've reread some of what I've written and it's all crap. I seem to be spending far too

Back in Aix

much time going over and over what I've written trying to make every word and every sentence perfect. I'm on week nine of The Artist's Way. Shouldn't my negative self-talk about my creative writing ability be eliminated by now? Shouldn't I just be able to turn up at the page and do the work without judging it?

I stop my morning pages mid-sentence and review the contract I'd made with myself when I first started *The Artist's Way*. I re-read some of the rules of the road. Three of them stick with me:

'Pray for guidance and courage and humility.'

'It's my job to do the work, not judge the work.'

'I will take care of the quantity, God will take care of the quality.'

I read them again, three times each. I finish my morning pages on a much more positive note.

My yoga practice this morning is focused and blissful, and the perfect mind and body boost for a day of writing. I sit down at my desk with a lovely salad and a clear head. Words escape me and they're captured on the page.

Billy arrives home from school for his standard snack lovingly purchased by me each day from the Boulangerie, Pauls.

Our after-school snack as kids was Weet-Bix smothered in butter and Vegemite. I ask him whether that would suffice for him when we get back to Melbourne.

"Not likely," he says, as a baguette with ham and cheese and a Flan Normand both disappear within minutes.

Dinner is with Chiara and Claudio at Pizzeria La Grange, en-route to the theatre. After the pizza pig-out in Italy I can barely manage one slice, even though it's supposed to be the best pizza in Aix.

It doesn't stop Billy, of course. He loves going out with these guys and seems to have formed a special friendship with Chiara, who is kind and liberal and full of funny stories about her own gorgeous son, Andrea. Both Claudio and Chiara treat Billy like a young adult, and he seems to shine in their presence.

Now at the Le Grande Theatre de Provence to see *Slava's Snowshow*, Billy appears pretty sceptical about it, especially given my recent live entertainment selections. We take our seats to see the famous show that's been staged by Russian Slava Polunin for many, many years on the world's greatest stages.

The curtains rise. The audience becomes silent. Smoke rolls across the floor as a lone sad clown shuffles onto the stage. It's Slava dressed in a bright yellow spacesuit with big red nose, sad drooping black eyes, wild frizzy hair and ridiculously oversized red shoes.

He's dragging a long red rope with a noose across the stage – a poignant and sad beginning. Other sad clowns with big droopy ears wearing deep green suits and gigantic shoes join him on stage.

Billy looks at me as if to say, 'I think I'm gonna like this.'

The clowns shuffle, roll and rumble to the music, and the lighting and the dazzling effects take us on a rollercoaster ride of make believe that is so real, every emotion is evoked, from sadness to joy, to hilarity and sadness again.

The show is unlike anything we've seen before. It 100 per cent deserves the standing ovation it gets.

As we leave, Billy says, "Thanks, Mum. That was the best show I've ever seen."

Hallelujah. Finally, I got it right.

Back in Aix

Wednesday 10 November
Aix

"Don't follow any advice, no matter how good, until you feel as deeply as in your spirit as you think in your mind that the counsel is wise." – *Joan Rivers*

I've organised a Skype session with Grace today. I want to talk to her about Billy and how I'm dealing with him. We have a very loving relationship and our communication is pretty good generally. I'm just tired of nagging him to get organised for school and to do his homework. I need some strategies to help him take responsibility for himself.

I've created a rod for my own back because I've done everything for him his whole life. It's not his fault. It's mine.

Grace and I discuss 'control issues'. I admit that for the last 10 years I've been 100 per cent in control of my whole life. I haven't had a boss to answer to or a life-partner to compromise with, and I've become very strong and independent. In a way, I've been the ruler of my own little kingdom with Billy my only subject. And now that subject is committing treason and I don't know how to deal with it.

We agree that the point of his time here in France is to get an education in life and that undone homework is unimportant in the scheme of things. After a long chat, I have a couple of really practical actions to take – the main one being to deliver instructions to him quietly face to face and only once and to then let go of the outcome. Proof, however, is going to be in the practice.

I write for the rest of the day until Billy comes home with three mates for a sleepover. He's really happy with his mates and I'm equally happy that there doesn't seem to be an ounce of potential treason in sight.

Thursday 11 November
Aix

> "Poetry is a deal of joy and pain and wonder, with a dash of the dictionary." – *Khalil Gibran*

Today I take my artist's date at Book in Bar. I'm keen to read more poetry, particularly from women poets, so I'm thrilled when I happen upon *Sixty Women Poets*. I buy it and settle down for a couple of hours with coffee in hand to absorb myself in the beautiful words. I'm struck by this poem.

Back in Aix

Standing Female Nude by Carol Ann Duffy

*Six hours like this for a few francs
Belly nipple arse in the window light
he drains the colour from me. Further to the right,
Madame. And do try to be still.
I shall be represented analytically and hung
in great museums. The bourgeoisie will coo
at such an image of a river-whore. They call it Art.*

*Maybe. He is concerned with volume, space.
I with the next meal. You're getting thin,
Madame, this is not good. My breasts hang
slightly low, the studio is cold. In the tea-leaves
I can see the Queen of England gazing
on my shape. Magnificent she murmurs
moving on. It makes me laugh. His name*

*is Georges. They tell me he's a genius.
There are times he does not concentrate
and stiffens for my warmth. Men think of their mothers.
He possesses me on canvas as he dips the brush
repeatedly into the paint. Little man,
you've not the money for the arts I sell.
Both poor, we make our living how we can.*

*I ask him Why do you do this? Because
I have to. There's no choice. Don't talk.
My smile confuses him. These Artists
take themselves too seriously. At night I fill myself
with wine and dance around the bars. When it's finished
he shows me proudly, lights a cigarette. I say
Twelve francs and get my shawl. It does not look like me.*

I love this poem from beginning to end. It evokes such vivid images of this poor resigned women being painted by a lonely suffering artist in a small squalid apartment somewhere in Montparnasse in Paris.

I wonder why I've gone so long without delving into poetry? Maybe I'll try my hand at writing poems after this book. What am I talking about? This book is my poetry!

My artist's date inspires me to write for the afternoon as I listen to Australian singer and songwriter Sarah Blasko's poetry set to music.

On Billy's return from school as evening approaches, we sit on the balcony with an aperitif, taking photos of birds on the wires with the brilliant pink sunset behind them. It's been a particularly artistic day today. My heart is light and my smile is soft.

⚜ ⚜ ⚜

Friday 12 November

Aix

"Attraction is not a choice."
– David DeAngelo

Back in Aix

The morning pages: *I feel really positive and excited about the future. I also feel hopeful about meeting a man that is right for me one day. The ad in Book in Bar was a complete failure. Can I be bothered taking any further action while I'm in France, or should I just enjoy my solitude, friends and writing? I'm not interested in creating a fairytale – Aussie girl meets French boy and falls madly in love – but it might be fun to have a couple of dates and flirtations.*

After Billy is off to school and I've done my run with Elizabeth, I meet Helen and Chiara for lunch at Toute une Histoire. We have a bawdy girly lunch and not even a drop of alcohol to fire it up. We share our respective love stories and stories of friends who've been both lucky and unlucky in love.

I'm just telling them about François when I receive a text. It's from him asking if I'd like to meet up again. I'm a little freaked out as I'd all but given up on him.

Chiara also tells me of the adventures of a friend of hers who's been using a French dating website called 'Meetic'. It sounds intriguing and I double-check the spelling just in case I'm tempted.

On my way home I text François: 'Okay let's meet again. When and where?'

I'm home at least five minutes before I sit down at my desk and type 'Meetic' into a search engine. Voilà! It's in front of me, all in French, of course.

At first glance there seems to be lots of very lovely men on it too. It might be a bit of fun and I'm game.

So instead of writing all afternoon, I spend it on Meetic. It's a big sacrifice to make for what's probably going to be a big waste of time. It takes me all afternoon as I laboriously complete my profile in French with the help of Google Translate. If nothing comes of it, at least I'm improving my language skills and having some fun.

Finally my profile is public. Within 30 minutes I have 10 emails. I didn't anticipate such a response so quickly. I decide that if they don't have a photo, speak English or live locally, I'll politely decline their offer. But now that I've set the wheels in motion, I won't look at any emails until tomorrow.

It's terribly amusing how the day's events have unfolded, especially considering the topic of my morning pages and our lunch. It reminds me how powerful thoughts and words truly can be.

Now writing is my priority. Men are completely forgotten.

⚜ ⚜ ⚜

Saturday 13 November
Aix

"Nothing in education is so astonishing as the amount of ignorance it accumulates in the form of inert facts." – *Henry Brooks Adams*

Back in Aix

I'm up at 6.45am – on a Saturday! I'm so committed to my morning pages now that I've set the alarm early enough to complete them before I get picked up by Helen to attend the parent/teacher interviews at school this morning.

I'm not making Billy go. I don't think he needs to be subjected to the negative comments sure to be thrust his way about his academic performance and given all he's had to contend with this year.

Also, I'm not very excited by the education system in general – learn what your teacher has taught you by rote, regurgitate it verbatim on paper, get a good mark and you're a star.

I feel passionately that a child should not be graded on his performance and pitted against his or her peers to fight for university places in order to study for a job that probably won't exist by the time he or she graduates. I believe education should be about inclusion and collaboration, not competition and that it desperately needs to evolve out of the industrialised world model. I believe our education system needs to nurture the whole of the child – spiritually, creatively, physically, emotionally and academically.

The meetings with the teachers go much as anticipated and I'm glad I left Billy at home in bed.

Lunch today is in St Marc Jaumegarde with Florence, Hugues, Jannick and Inés. This beautiful scenic area of Provence is just 15 minutes east of Aix and close to the glorious Mount Saint-Victoire, the fabulous mountain that can be seen from our apartment rooftop.

Lunch is a traditional Alsace dish, Choucroute Garnie. Onions and garlic are cooked in duck fat before adding in sauerkraut, juniper berries, bay leaves, caraway seeds, black pepper, stock and finally a very healthy splash of Alsace Riesling. Finally potatoes, pork ribs, ham and Polish sausage are thrown in to complete this comforting, homey winter dish. It's absolutely delicious and the Pinot Gris accompanying it makes for a taste sensation.

After lunch, there's nothing for it but a walk up the mountain and along the ancient ridge-top trail to take in the glorious views over Aix and Mount Saint-Victoire.

We reach the peak and look out over Aix far below us, as the sun is beginning to set. It illuminates the sky with a range of colours alternating between brilliant gold, burnt orange and pastel pink.

I leave the others for a few minutes to take it in and retreat into my own private space. After taking a photo, I tilt my face towards the sun, open my chest and allow the heat of the diminishing rays to warm my eyes, face and throat and pierce my heart. We walk home in blissful silence. After that sunset, there's really not much to say.

Back in Aix

Sunday 14 November
Aix

> "One who has control over the mind is tranquil in heat and cold, in pleasure and pain, and in honour and dishonour and is ever steadfast with the Supreme Self." – *Bhagavad Gita*

Sunday. Not a complete day of rest, but still gorgeous.

I have a light run and then coffee with Andrew and Elizabeth before attending a fabulous yoga workshop with a visiting Californian yoga guru, Mark Holzman, who's just moved lock, stock and barrel from LA to Paris. He tells us stories, reads some beautiful pieces from his collection of poems and entices us into some neat new poses.

I'm totally limber and relaxed when I get home. As Billy studies for exams, I write. At dinner over a sumptuous curry, we just chat about stuff. Some of it's important. Some of it's not. The connection, not the content, is what sustains us.

Monday 15 November

Aix

"Fill the paper with the breathings of your heart."
– *William Wordsworth*

It's book month at Billy's school and I've been invited to speak to six consecutive classes on 'How to write a book'.

My mission today is to simply inspire the students to write, not just books, anything; short stories, speeches, articles poems, songs, screen plays, whatever.

Billy is totally embarrassed about it and equally embarrassed that I'm riding the school bus with him. I have strict instructions to be the last one on the bus, to sit at the front and not talk to him. I decide to comply. I would've done exactly the same thing to my mother at that age.

It's been over six months since my last public speaking gig and I'm concerned I might've lost my mojo. I've also never taught kids before – a far more daunting prospect than teaching adults.

As the first class enters the library, I take a big deep breath and conjure up a winning smile. Within a few minutes the words are flowing and the engagement seems high.

When Billy arrives with his classmates, I'm extra nervous. He appears to be closely monitoring their faces and comments to gauge their reaction to the lesson. I'm unsure if he'll

Back in Aix

ask me a smart-arse question to stir things up but thankfully the lesson is incident free.

As the day progresses, the classes are filled with older students and they become even more engaged. I feel more and more in my element as I end each class with this quote.

'The idea is to write it so people hear it and it slides through the brain and goes straight to the heart." – *Anon*

They leave with a handout: Top 20 Tips to Writing a Book.
1. Write, write, write – about anything!
2. Choose a topic and theme you're passionate about.
3. Set a deadline and date for the book to be published.
4. Imagine yourself launching the book.
5. Share your goal with someone you trust.
6. Hang out with other writers.
7. Read the books of the writers you love.
8. Do a creative writing course.
9. Map out the structure and table of contents.
10. Set small daily writing objectives.
11. Discover your most productive writing habits – daily and weekly.
12. Decide if you're going to self-publish or find a publisher.
13. Prepare a book proposal for the publisher.
14. Don't be a perfectionist.
15. Don't judge your work, just do it.
16. Find a brilliant editor.
17. Consider how to market your book – blog, website, speaking, publicity.
18. Have fun with it.

19. Write with authenticity, passion and a belief in yourself.
20. Don't wait! Take one small step every day.

At the end of the day as I head across the gravel car park to hop on the bus, I'm fully appreciative of the enthusiasm of the students and equally appreciative of what it must take to be an engaging teacher.

I sit up the front of the bus as requested while my son is somewhere up the back chatting with his friends and totally ignoring me.

I'm not bothered. I know he's secretly quite happy and proud of me. A mother can sense these things a mile away.

⚜ ⚜ ⚜

Tuesday 16 November
Aix

"If you are afraid of loneliness, do not marry."
– *Anton Chekhov*

Today's morning pages are once again a tribute to women. After listing all the names of the women I know and love, I

Back in Aix

reflect on their lives. Some have brought up their children singlehandedly with little or no support. Others have never had children despite a deep desire to. Others are stuck in a marriage they can't seem to escape from. Others are single like me and desire a committed partnership. And yet others are happily married and content. No matter what their circumstance, loneliness has struck each of these women at sometime during their life.

I'm reminded of a poem and go searching for it on the internet. It's an ode to a man, written by a woman called Oriah Mountaindreamer. It's a far more eloquent call for love and commitment than my own words will ever be. As I copy it in my journal in my large flowing handwriting, I feel every word of it deep in my heart.

Invitation by Oriah

It doesn't interest me
what you do for a living.
I want to know
what you ache for
and if you dare to dream
of meeting your heart's longing.
It doesn't interest me
how old you are.
I want to know
if you will risk
looking like a fool
for love
for your dream
for the adventure of being alive.

UNSTUCK IN PROVENCE

*It doesn't interest me
what planets are
squaring your moon
I want to know
if you have touched
the centre of your own sorrow
if you have been opened
by life's betrayals
or have become shrivelled and closed
from fear of further pain.
I want to know
if you can sit with pain
without moving to hide it
or fade it
or fix it.
I want to know
if you can be with joy
mine or your own
if you can dance with wildness
and let the ecstasy fill you
to the tips of your fingers and toes
without cautioning us
to be careful
to be realistic
to remember the limitations
of being human.
It doesn't interest me
if the story you are telling me
is true.
I want to know if you can
disappoint another*

Back in Aix

to be true to yourself.
If you can bear
the accusation of betrayal
and not betray your own soul.
If you can be faithless
and therefore trustworthy.
I want to know if you can see beauty
even when it is not pretty
every day.
And if you can source your own life
from its presence.
I want to know
if you can live with failure
yours and mine
and still stand at the edge of the lake
and shout to the silver of the full moon,
"Yes."
It doesn't interest me
to know where you live
or how much money you have.
I want to know if you can get up
after a night of grief and despair
weary and bruised to the bone
and do what needs to be done
to feed the children.
It doesn't interest me
who you know
or how you came to be here.
I want to know if you will stand
in the centre of the fire
with me

*and not shrink back.
It doesn't interest me
where or what or with whom
you have studied.
I want to know
what sustains you
from the inside
when all else falls away.*

Morning Pages. Yoga. Writing. Lunch. Writing. The routine is comforting.

The only break to the routine is a coffee with François. He's enchanting and very pleasant to converse with, but there's no spark, and of course, he's married. I'm friendly and polite yet somewhat detached. There are far more important things on the boil.

Aperitif. Dinner. Mother and son time. Bed. More writing. It's my happy, happy lot in life.

Back in Aix

Wednesday 17 November
Aix

"Go with the flow." – *Proverb*

After Billy is off to school, I run with Elizabeth. I'm starting to really love this running business! At home I write. I eat lunch. I write. I cook dinner. I write. I go to bed. I still can't stop writing. It's still my happy, happy lot in life.

Thursday 18 November
Aix to Marseille

"Are we to paint what's on the face, what's inside the face or what's behind it?" – *Pablo Picasso*

I squeeze in two hours of writing before heading off with Chiara, Andrew, Elizabeth and Helen to Marseille, the second biggest city of France and just a 25-minute bus trip from Aix.

Our entrance into Marseille is in stark contrast to our entrance into Aix some months ago. Hundreds of homeless people are huddled around a huge smouldering fire in their self-designated camping ground. Makeshift tents, old shopping trolleys and steaming piles of rubbish mark their territory.

It's a very sad scene that stays with me as we stroll around the old port, full of vessels flanked by two large forts – Saint-Nicolas and Saint-Jean.

We trek up the hill to La Basilique Notre Dame de la Garde, the huge Neo-Byzantine church built atop the brilliant white limestone cliffs. The Notre Dame, the 'good mother', is the protector of the city. It's easy to see why, with its 360-degree views.

The inside of this cathedral is haunting and incredibly warm and human. Its glittering gold domes are inlaid with mosaics of peacocks and angels, and the walls are adorned with photographs depicting the sea, land and air disasters of the region. Tiny models of boats and planes hang on invisible lines dropping down from the ceiling. It's simply breathtaking.

In the Bay of Marseille there's the Frioul Archipelago, four small islands – one of which bears the Chateau d'If. This huge fortress, originally built for defence, became the most notorious and feared prison in France, made famous by Dumas in *The Count of Monte Cristo*.

It's nearing dusk. At a charity art event being hosted by a friend of Chiara's, we push our way into the throngs of people eagerly surveying the hundreds of miniature paintings by

France's most popular artists. They're all for sale at just 111 Euro each.

I've never really had much of an eye for art, so I take my time and study each piece in detail. That's when I happen upon her, a drawing and painting combination of a woman. Her eyes are closed, her face impassive and unreadable. She's bare breasted and her arms are held forward in a ballerina like pose. Her hips are encased in bright red robes, ready to fall at any moment. I love her. I buy her. I name her the Mistress of Marseille.

Friday 19 November
Aix

"Rudeness is the weak man's imitation of strength." – *Eric Hoffer*

The thought of a day ahead of me writing in this beautiful place thrills me. I love putting words together and having them conjure up images of things, of people, of places and emotions. I can't wait to spend the day writing. Get to it! That's how I end my morning pages.

I head out the door for a run as Billy heads off to school. At home I write. I will, I will achieve my goal!

At 5pm I'm loitering outside La Rotonde Bar in the frosty cold waiting for Michel, my Meetic date. Each time a lone man walks past, I scan his face for any resemblance to his profile photo. At 5.15 there's no sign of him. I text him to let him know I'm here. No response.

By 5.25 he still hasn't arrived.

'F**k you, Michel. You're a rude bastard,' I curse to myself as I enter the bar, perch myself on a stool and order Champagne.

I feel dejected and angry. I need some girly support. I text my friend Julie in the US to share my sad state of affairs. Her response? "Remember the scene in *Sex and the City*, where Carrie stands up Miranda for Big? Miranda is left in the bar drinking on her own, and she meets Steve the bartender, her future husband. What's the bartender like?"

I giggle aloud and text back "She's a woman and I'm not quite that disenchanted with men that I'd turn to women… yet. ☺"

Dressed up and dateless, I sip my drink in this purple-hued, dark-wood, chandeliered den for meeting men. Perhaps my Higher Power is sending me a huge message. 'Wrong time. Wrong place.'

Back in Aix

Saturday 20 November
Aix

"To love oneself is the beginning of a life-long romance."
– Oscar Wilde

I vent in my morning pages. *I'm pissed off at that guy Michel for not turning up and having the decency to contact me. It's just so rude. Maybe he did turn up, take one look and leave. Whatever his reason, it's rude!*

Then the pages turn more positive. *It's nice actually not having a man occupying my mind. It's been a long time since that's happened. It's only been a few months since the affair with James ended. Maybe I'm not meant to have a lover here. Maybe I need to build my own self-love and self-worth before seeking love from another?*

I've been on Meetic one week and have received 30 emails. To be frank, with my three filters in play for vetting my suitors, it's not turning up much talent. How could it be in this love-crazed nation? I've also carefully avoided searching and initiating contact myself. I'm aware how time-consuming online dating can be, and my writing is way too important. Is that saying something?

Our comforting and enjoyable Saturday routine takes over.

After our taste test tour and market purchases, Billy and I take up residence at our cosy corner table at our favourite café, Brasserie de L'Horloge (Café Clock). We observe the hustle and bustle of the markets and tune into the romantic French accents floating all around us as we sip our customary café crème and chocolat chaud.

It really does feel like heaven right here on earth.

⚜ ⚜ ⚜

Aix

"Keep your dreams alive. Understand to achieve anything requires faith and belief in yourself, vision, hard work, determination and dedication. Remember all things are possible for those who believe."
– *Gail Devers*

The stats look like this: 25,541 words written, about 40,000 words to go and 41 days to achieve it. Is it possible? Perhaps a little bit of my new music love, Lucy Schwartz, a young LA-born indie singer and songwriter, will get me fired up for the day.

Back in Aix

Monday 22 November
Aix

"Christmas is not a time nor a season, but a state of mind. To cherish peace and goodwill, to be plenteous in mercy is to have the real spirit of Christmas."
– Calvin Coolidge

As I return home from my run along the main street of Aix, along Cours Mirabeau, I'm amazed at its transformation. With just a month until Christmas, the strip has been turned into a total Tinsel Town. There's a series of little wooden huts erected along the whole strip selling everything from gaudy tree decorations to nativity scene statues.

Every tree and fountain is adorned with lights, decorations and fake snow, and the business owners appear to be in aggressive competition to win the *Most Over-The-Top Window Award*. Carols blast out of big speakers strategically placed at intervals to ensure you'll enjoy the music at every point along the strip.

It's all highly commercial and rather tacky. No wonder people go silly and overspend at this time of year. In this environment anyone would be hard pressed to resist. There's not much chance I'll succumb though, as Billy will be home before Christmas, leaving me here on my own.

For a brief moment I'm a little sad that I won't be spending Christmas with him. Then I consider how wonderful it'll be for him to be reunited with his father and his step-mum, both of whom he's missed terribly.

And on my own, I'll be able to play the role of reclusive novelist in my cosy little artist's retreat right here in Aix! Nice, really.

⚜ ⚜ ⚜

Tuesday 23 November
Aix

"Yoga is invigoration in relaxation. Freedom in routine. Confidence through self-control. Energy within and without." – *Ymber Delecto*

The Artist's Way is asking me to read my old morning pages, something that until now had been dissuaded. I'm not keen. I'm a little scared of regressing back to the state I was in many weeks ago when I'd first started. Stuffing the first of my journals in my bag, I decide that I'll read it later somehow, somewhere – if I must.

The temperature has been dropping significantly over the last month, so I wrap myself up well for the walk to yoga. Yoga has been a big contributor to my state of mind and happiness and I wonder why I'd let it slip in Sydney.

On the journey home, I take a detour into a quiet little unpopulated café and order a coffee. Tentatively I open my bag and place my journal before me. I remind myself not to judge it as I open to the first page.

After about an hour and 30 pages into it, I stop to reflect. There are many pages filled with rants about James and my lack of sound judgement and self-esteem around men generally. I'm bemused at how clearly love-addicted I'd been.

I feel none of that right now – not one little bit. Right now, compared to then, I feel, um, free.

⚜ ⚜ ⚜

Wednesday 24 November
Aix to Marseille

"The people who run our cities don't understand graffiti because they think nothing has the right to exist unless it makes a profit. The people who truly deface our neighborhoods are the companies that scrawl giant slogans across buildings and buses trying to make us feel inadequate unless we buy their stuff." – *Banksy*

Billy is off to school this morning happy and excited at the prospect of seeing *Harry Potter and the Deathly Hallows* this afternoon – in English! While I'm out running I decide to have a morning of artistic endeavor at Book in Bar.

A book sitting on the shelf next to me catches my eye. It's Banksy's *Wall and Piece*. I'm immediately intrigued by this unidentified British graffiti artist whose stencil work has appeared all over the world.

Banksy is well known for his contempt for the government for labelling graffiti as vandalism merely because it doesn't provide a profit. The book is filled with photos of his graffiti stencils, featuring striking, thought-provoking and humorous images and slogans.

His messages are anti-war, anti-capitalist and anti-establishment, and his subjects are rats, monkeys, policemen and soldiers. It's a brilliant book and I admire his courage to stand firmly against mainstream society.

Now it's Harry Potter time! Billy arrives at the last minute with Helen, Owen and Merlin just as the curtains part. We're enthralled from start to finish.

"What did you think?" I ask Billy.

"It was good but not as good as the book, and Emma Watson is really hot."

I laugh as I realise that this kid is definitely not the same kid I took to the last Harry Potter movie!

Billy is having a night at Helen's while Andrew, Elizabeth and I are off to see Canadian indie rock band Arcade Fire at Le Dome in Marseille. Their music has been inspiring my writing for quite a few weeks, so I'm excited to be seeing them in the flesh on French territory.

Back in Aix

Comfortably seated in the pavilion, the eight band members run onto the elaborate stage. There's every standard instrument amongst some highly unusual ones – the glockenspiel, harp, mandolin and finally a hurdy-gurdy. They're the most talented and versatile bunch of musicians I've ever seen. The crowd erupts over and over as they jump from one instrument to another and play hit after hit. They finish with their classic, 'Wake Up' and the chants of the audience reverberate around the stadium, bringing the whole evening to a dramatic climax. I really do love live music!

We leave Le Dome to find a taxi or a train to take us back to Aix. As we walk along what appears to be a major road it's getting quieter and more deserted.

We'd been warned Marseille is a hotspot for theft and crime, particularly at night, so by now all senses are on full alert. Arriving at the metro station, hoping to catch the last train back to Aix, we find the doors locked and rats running along the escalator rails inside.

"What's our plan?" asks Andrew.

"I suggest we go back to the venue," I say. "At least there'll be other people there."

We return along the road from whence we came and the hairs on the back of my neck stand up. Three young men, out on the prowl, strut toward us on the other side of the road. We pick up the pace, eyes straight ahead and thank God when they ignore us.

Finally we reach the venue to discover a few patient policemen providing security for a small group of stranded concertgoers. Only then do the three of us take a deep breath and crack a smile at each other.

Finally, 30 minutes later, we secure what must be the last taxi open for business and a driver that's willing to take us back to Aix. Phew!

Thursday 25 November
Aix

"There are two kinds of women in the world; one who wants power in the world, and one who wants power in the bed." – *Jacqueline Kennedy Onassis*

I'm tired after last night. *Is it okay to stay in bed all day and write?'* I ask my morning pages.

Yes, they answer. So I do, and the words flow just as powerfully as if I was showered and dressed sitting at my little red writing desk.

Back in Aix

Friday 26 November
Aix

"Food for the body is not enough. There must be food for the soul." – Dorothy Day

Today I've decided that eating out with friends and pampering are going to take precedence over writing. Why have I allowed this to happen twice in one week? Because I can. Make the most of it… I write.

Billy is staying with Henry tonight. I have a day and night to myself. Bliss.

A fast and vigorous run around La Torse before a luxurious pedicure and manicure, a simple moules et frite (mussels with French Fries) lunch and a spot of shopping with Florence fill this most glorious day.

After a catnap I meet Andrew and Elizabeth for an aperitif at La Rotonde, the scene of my no-show date with Michel. They're amused by my story and console me over a sumptuous dinner at La Tomate Verte – foie gras, canard (duck) and chocolat tarte.

Bundled up in my thick, warm coat, I meander home slowly to take in the Christmas lights and wonder if perhaps they're not that gaudy after all. It's actually quite beautiful and serene, without all the crowds and the Christmas carols, that is. The novelty of being in this gorgeous city in this gorgeous country has still not worn off. I hop into bed, alone as usual, and it really feels quite okay.

⚜ ⚜ ⚜

Saturday 27 November
Aix

"To market, to market, to buy a fat pig,
Home again, home again, jiggety-jig"
– *Mother Goose*

For some inexplicable reason the words of this childhood rhyme spring to mind as I swing downstairs to the markets. When Billy was a baby just six months old, I'd bounce him repeatedly on my knee and sing him this song. It's a heart-warming albeit distant memory.

As I mingle amongst the market crowd and soak up the atmosphere, I hop from one familiar stall to another collecting my produce. There are no whole fat pigs for sale, but a nice piece of warm roast pork catches my attention.

Billy walks in the door.

"How was your night, mate?"

"Great. I'm tired. We were on the computer until 1am. I'm going to have a sleep this afternoon. But first I'm starving. What is there to eat?"

Priceless. This boy has just summed up his three most precious pastimes in one monologue – computers, sleeping and eating.

As I prepare lunch, something outside the window catches my eye. Soft swirly snowflakes are drifting by.

We race to the window and thrust our hands out to catch some flakes. It makes our whole artist's retreat even cosier as we eat and chat about nothing in particular.

As Billy rests in the loft above me, I engage my brain and employ my fingers. I look up regularly from the keyboard to watch the snowflakes eddy and flow. I'm happier than I've been in years.

Sunday 28 November
Aix

"We only part to meet again." – *John Gay*

While Billy spends the day supposedly studying for exams, I write, of course.

Later that evening, Andrew and Elizabeth drop over to say goodbye. They're leaving tomorrow. Billy and I are both really very sad. They've become great friends and we share a similar philosophy on life, not to mention a passion for music and food.

We toast to our good health and safe travels. Then they hand me a bottle of Champagne with strict instructions not to open it until I write the last word of my book on 1 January 2011.

We're all teary as they leave. At least there's some comfort in the fact that it's only a matter of months before we'll see them back in Melbourne.

⚜ ⚜ ⚜

Monday 29 November
Aix

"Happiness lies in the joy of achievement and the thrill of creative effort." – *Franklin D. Roosevelt*

Today I create an artist's altar on the corner of my little red writing desk. On it is the bottle of Champagne from Andrew and Elizabeth, the yellow card with the affirmation I wrote some months ago and the purple card with my action plan. There's also a card with my yoga chant on it, a couple of exquisite old postcards and Billy's birthday card to me.

My artist's altar spurs me on. It feeds my creativity and fuels my writing.

I put on Ron – Ron Sexsmith, Canadian singer and songwriter of the exact same vintage as me. Cool name. Cool man. Damn cool music to write to.

Tuesday 30 November
Aix

"If you do not breathe through writing, if you do not cry out in writing, or sing in writing, then don't write, because our culture has no use for it."
– Anais Nin

The morning pages again.

I've become 100 per cent committed to these morning pages. I think I've missed only one day since I started the program. I love the discipline of them. They've made me cry and they've made me laugh at myself. They've helped me tap into my deepest creative juices.

They've motivated me to write. They've helped me work through the pain of unrequited love and the fear of uncertainty around my future. They've helped me heal. They've helped me find peace.

Another day in my perfectly happy routine. Billy to school. Hot chocolate in bed while writing the morning pages. Yoga. Breakfast. Coffee. Writing. Lunch. Coffee. Writing. Dinner. Homework. Movie. Writing. Bed. Boring? Never!

6
The Beginning of the End
Aix en Provence

Wednesday 1 December
Aix

> "I have always found that my view of success has been iconoclastic: success to me is not about money or status or fame, it's about finding a livelihood that brings me joy and self-sufficiency and a sense of contributing to the world." – *Anita Roddick*

Billy leaves reluctantly for school. He has exams this week and, it appears, girl trouble. That's two big reasons it takes extra coaxing from me to get him going this morning.

I close the door behind him and jump into bed to start my morning pages. I've barely begun and my phone rings.

"Mum, I've missed the bus."

When he returns home, it's clear it was a deliberate ploy to play hooky. I'm not happy and make it known. His penance is to clean his loft and two hours of study.

I have another Skype session with Grace this morning to discuss my future livelihood and my business. I haven't been thinking much about it, but now that it's only a month before I'll be back in Melbourne, the reality of the need to earn an income is starting to make me panic a little.

While I know that my livelihood has to have meaning and purpose and make a difference to others, that's pretty much all I have to go on. After a long chat with Grace I decide that panic is pointless and to just relish every last day, hour, minute and second of my time here in this beautiful country.

Turning my annoyance at Billy into some overdue love and attention, we enjoy a delectable lunch of bread, olives, tapenade, ham, cheese and salad together and chat about school, his friends (and his girl problems), what he'll miss about France and what he's looking forward to in Melbourne.

He's somehow different, this kid who came to France from Sydney as a child on the cusp of his teenage years. He seems to have matured into a young man right before my very eyes.

Thursday 2 December

Aix

"The first rule of magic is self-containment. Hold your intention within yourself stocking it with power. Only then will you be able to manifest your desire." – *Julia Cameron*

I have just one month before I leave Aix to start a totally new chapter of my life. I still have much to do and see, and much to write. I'm on week 12, the final week of *The Artist's Way*. It feels like I'm about to lose my best friend. I make a snap decision not to finish it, just yet.

My final month here will be spent reviewing all the chapters, pulling out the pearls of wisdom and rewriting my affirmations and goals in my moleskine journal. I'm going to stock my desires and intentions with power, complete chapter 12 in my final week here in Aix, and write a new contract to myself on 1 January.

I write with focus and intent all day, totally uninterrupted until Billy rings the buzzer at the end of the day.

"We've broken up. This time it's for good," he tells me breathlessly after running up the stairs two at a time.

"How do you feel?" I ask him.

"It's okay. It's not because I'm leaving. It just wasn't working."

He's so upset about it that he can't wait to get on Facebook and share the news.

"So much for grieving in solitude," I laugh.

"I might be a bit sadder when I go to bed tonight," he responds. "In the meantime, did you get me a baguette and an éclair?"

His first love begins and ends right here in France. Sweet.

The Beginning of the End

Friday 3 December
Aix

"True enjoyment comes from activity of the mind and exercise of the body; the two are united."
– Alexander von Humbolt

I remember how bad I felt as I was writing about James for the book some weeks ago. It was really tough reliving that experience all over again. And then yesterday I had to write about the trip to see John. That was tough, too. All the feelings I had just came back up again. I feel okay today, though. Cleansed somehow. I don't really have any interest in meeting a man in France now. There are too many other delicious things to enjoy and focus on until I leave.

Billy is staying the night at Henry's again. It's fun for him, fun for Henry and good for Billy and I to have time out from each other. I just hope Henry's mum finds it fun too. It must be okay if he keeps getting invited back.

I meet Florence and her friend Marc at La Rotonde for an aperitif. I've been told he's a 'Meetic freak' so I'm hoping she's not trying to set me up with him.

We converse in a curious Frenglish mix with Florence interpreting from time to time. Drinks are followed by dinner at Chez Mitch, one of the top restaurants in Aix. We're escorted downstairs to the cave where the wine is stored and the tables are elegantly set. The ambience is soft, warm and cosy, and the food is delicious – crab and prawn entrée, lamb on risotto and crème caramel accompanied by a carefully selected vin rouge.

The conversation is equally delicious as Marc regales us with his various dating stories. If he's a typical French man, I'm glad I've kept my chastity here. He's funny and I like him, and it's good to have the inside information on Meetic.

Walking home alone and full to the brim, I thank God I've rediscovered running here. I just don't understand how the men and women of this country stay so thin, especially as exercise – of the vertical type at least – doesn't seem to be high on their agenda.

♣ ♣ ♣

Saturday 4 December
Aix

"No party is any fun unless seasoned with folly."
– *Desiderius Erasmus*

Today I feel a little sad and fearful. I'm not sure why. Is it because I'm uncertain of my future? Is it because I feel sluggish from all

The Beginning of the End

the food last night? I'm not sure. Don't judge it, Carolyn. It will pass, like every feeling passes.

I love writing. I was meant to write, no matter how good or bad my words are. I'm a channel for my Higher Power. What does my Higher Power even look like?

I've no idea how the pages lead me to this point. I've long ago given up wondering about that.

When it comes to God, I still visualise a brown-haired, brown-bearded man in flowing white robes and sandals. It's the God of my youth, not the God of my life now. I'm keen to replace the old vision with a new vision of my Higher Power.

I take a long drink of water and get comfortable before I go into a deep meditation. After what seems like an eternity, I've conjured up an image of her.

She's within me and around me, and so is her love. Her luminous face is suspended above mine and she's smiling gently almost in bemusement. She's sensuous, beautiful, dark-skinned and dark-haired. Her bright flowing garments envelope me and provide a protective shield while her arms encircle me and her hands are pressed gently together in front of me.

Namaste. I salute you.

She's whispering to me. She asks me to have faith, to surrender and to let her be my guide. She asks me to release my judgements of the past and my fears about the future. She asks me to embrace and accept all people and all religions, to show deep love and compassion to others and to myself.

I've no idea how long I meditate on her. I awake some time later to write down everything I can recall about her. When I've finished I can't really feel her presence, but I do feel serene and at peace.

Then I feel a little stupid and laugh at myself. It might take some time to get used to this new vision of my invisible friend, my Higher Power.

Billy is still at Henry's, so I have a glorious day to myself. It's much like every other Saturday, minus Billy. Run. Yoga. Markets.

I love the antique markets and the clothing markets around Place des Precheurs, so I wander aimlessly for an hour or so buying bits and pieces and a few gifts for friends.

When I've had enough, I sit in another of my favourite cafés, Brasserie L'Unic overlooking Place Richelme, munching on a salad niçoise, writing in my moleskine and reading my poetry book.

I arrive home at the same time as Billy and we spend a couple of hours together until we're collected by Richie and Agnés for a wine and cheese degustation at their home in Venelles.

I'm a bit nervous about how we're going to manage conversation in a room full of native French people. Within five minutes my fears are allayed. It's immediately obvious most of them speak far better English than I'll ever speak French. That doesn't stop me, though. I still try as best I can.

Throughout the evening we're treated to wines from almost every year and every corner of France. We sniff. We taste. We talk. We happily munch our way through Richie's homemade foie gras, porc terrines and every kind of fromage imaginable.

As the wine flows, we're getting louder and more boisterous. Childhood songs are played with gusto on guitar and are accompanied by spoon-playing and soulful, wine-soaked voices. The younger children are following Billy around as though he's the Pied Piper, until they all head off to bed.

The Beginning of the End

It's 1am when I tread lightly upstairs to wake Billy up for our ride home. I feel sorry for him as he grumbles and stumbles to his feet. When we arrive home he settles down to sleep and I crawl exhausted into my own bed and reflect on the evening's events.

We could not have been more graciously embraced and welcomed by these friendly and fun French natives. The evening had also reminded me how much I love a party and meeting new people. J'adore la France!

Sunday 5 December
Aix

"Sleep is the best meditation." – Dalai Lama

Today's morning pages are happy and light and done in no time. I'm not yet ready to write my book, so update our blog, *The Daily Slice of French Life*. It starts like this: 'It's 9.37am. I'm writing this blog snuggled up in my bed in my cosy room. A freshly brewed cup of coffee sits on my bedside table, which is piled high with books and three overflowing journals filled with my musings from the first day we arrived in Paris. There's a lamp on my bedside table. Its shade is perched at an angle and it bathes my room with a soft, gentle light. The mellow, sensuous voice of Lloyd Cole is serenading me as I write. My son is still fast asleep in the loft upstairs in our warm, earthy artist's retreat in the heart of Aix en Provence. I know that it's extremely cold outside but it doesn't matter to me right now. Perhaps when I decide to pluck up the courage to go for a run, it will matter.'

An hour later I've published our blog, which has actually become a 'weekly slice' due to various other writing distractions.

Billy is still sleeping, so I neatly segue into book writing. Three hours later, Billy is still sleeping and I've produced another thousand words, and before I know it, the day is over. I never do venture outside for that run. Oh well.

⚜ ⚜ ⚜

Monday 6 December
Aix

"The hottest love has the coldest end." – *Socrates*

I feel strange and unsettled today. I had a dream that I was in a shop and talking to the woman behind the counter when James walked in. I looked at him and he looked straight through me at

The Beginning of the End

the woman serving me. She told me she was going out on a date with him tonight. I said something pleasant enough, turned on my heel and walked out without looking back. It was so vivid, this dream, that it woke me up... I write in my morning pages.

I put on a happy face until Billy leaves for school and then go back to bed for a while and continue to reflect on this dream that was so short, yet so real. I'm convinced that it's just one more step in the process of totally letting go. The only remedy is running, reading and a whole lot of writing.

Tuesday 7 December
Aix

> "In times of sickness the soul collects itself anew."
> – *Latin Proverb*

I feel unwell today. Snotty nose. Heavy eyes. Aching body. Maybe I've been overdoing the running in this cold weather? It's okay to feel unwell. It happens. Don't judge it.

Braving yoga, I attempt to eliminate the sick cells in my body with some intense 'Oms' and salutes to the sun. On the way home I stop off for my café at Happy Days, buy some produce from the markets and Billy's standard after-school snack and visit one of my favourite vintage clothing stores. I buy some very cool second-hand Italian snow boots. A little unconventional retail therapy is just the motivation I need to write for the rest of the day.

⚜ ⚜ ⚜

Wednesday 8 December
Aix

"I'm not concerned with your liking or disliking me... all I ask is that you respect me as a human being." – *Jackie Robinson*

I'm giving Meetic, very half-heartedly, one last go. I've had numerous emails from Loic, who seems nice and worthy of a coffee at least. I respond to his third email and give him my phone number. He calls me and we arrange to meet on Monday at the 'den for meeting men', La Rotonde.

But that's next week and the now is all I care about, as I visit the markets to buy fresh produce to cook dinner for Chiara

The Beginning of the End

and Claudio – foie gras de canard, scallops, monk fish, prawns, beetroot, rocket, cheeses and breads.

At least for today, I'll pretend I can cook. I'm going to fake it and hope I make it. I'm courageously (or perhaps stupidly) attempting a seafood risotto for these two Italian foodies.

We have a really fun evening with them both, listening to music, eating, drinking, laughing and telling stories. And the risotto? Sadly it's not one of my best cooking performances, but at least edible. Our guests leave. Our beds are beckoning. The cleaning up can wait until the morning.

⚜ ⚜ ⚜

Thursday 9 December
Aix

> "We define therapy as search for value."
> – *Abraham Maslow*

So far since arriving in France I've deliberately censored myself from all mainstream media such as television, radio, magazines and papers and all its harshness. I've chosen to spend my leisure time pursuing more positive, spiritual and creative activities such as reading books, listening to music, going on my artist's dates and writing (in all its forms).

This week there's been one exception. I've discovered, thanks to my sister Di, the television series *In Treatment*, and I'm hooked. It stars Gabriel Byrne, who plays a therapist called Paul. As he treats his own patients he also receives therapy to help him through his own mid-life crisis and marriage break-up. It's all rather complex and deeply fascinating and insightful.

I love the way he asks questions, listens, acknowledges his patients' pain and helps them arrive at their own solutions.

And now therapy has become the topic of my morning pages.

I'm so grateful for Grace and the support she has given me. She brought to light my patterns of love addiction to James and other men. She's helped me remain positive and hopeful and she's spurred me into action. Thanks to her I've been able to make some big life-changing decisions. I've also learnt an incredible array of skills from her in how to be compassionate and a good questioner and listener with my clients and girlfriends. I wish everyone could have easy and inexpensive access to a therapist like Paul or my own Grace.

My cold is still lurking around, which gives me just the excuse I need to stay in bed all day and write. The process of writing and the progress I'm making keeps me inspired until 5pm. That's when I decide I should get up and shower before I find myself with some very unattractive and painful bed sores.

Billy comes home and we enjoy a beautiful Korean barbecue dinner at a local restaurant, something totally un-French. I love it when the two of us have dinner out together. It's when we're most connected because there are no distractions. We talk about our day, girls, friends, family and Melbourne. It's really, really nice.

The Beginning of the End

Friday 10 December
La Bastide-des-Jourdans

> "Mothers are the necessity of invention."
> — *Bill Watterson*

I'm suffering. I have a cold. It doesn't seem to be getting better or worse. It just lurks. I feel clogged up and aching from head to toe. What shall I do? Stop whinging, get up and have a shower, go to the markets and just write.

And that's exactly what I do until 2.30pm. Thank God for the morning pages.

We're staying the weekend with Helen, Merlin and Owen at their lovely home at La Bastide-des-Jourdans in Vaucluse (in southeast France, not Sydney's east) and in the Luberon National Park. Helen collects me from the rotunda and we pick up the boys from school on the way home.

Billy and I can't wait to get to their place to see Chloe and her seven one-week old-puppies. Chloe is a lovely caramel-coloured cocker spaniel that had unexpectedly become pregnant to the neighbouring Labrador.

The puppies' eyes are still closed and they pull themselves along on their tummies, sniffing, squealing and searching for their mother's milk. Their coats are a beautiful sand colour and they're all perfectly formed.

If they're cute now, I can only imagine how cute they're going to be in a few weeks when they open their eyes and start to walk. Their mother is very attentive, ensuring each pup is being fed and that we're handling her precious babies with care as we cuddle each one in turn. It's a wonderfully life-affirming experience.

⚜ ⚜ ⚜

Saturday 11 December
La Bastide-des-Jourdans

"The answers to life's problems aren't at the bottom of a bottle, they're on TV." – *Homer Simpson*

It's a slow start this morning for us all after a delicious dinner and a late night of watching movies.

I write my book in bed for a few hours before we get up. I'm still not feeling that well and can't seem to shake this damn cold.

It's a beautiful crisp sunshiny day as we take a drive through the Luberon to Lourmarin, walk around the shops and have lunch at a very traditional French-international bistro. The

The Beginning of the End

escargot in mushroom sauce and stuffed bone marrow are to die for and are followed by the obligatory crème brûlée.

I marvel at how exquisite Lourmarin is and can fully understand why it's frequented by the rich and famous. The light and colours in this area are ethereal, the scenery is exquisite, and the shops and restaurants are superb.

I love that we're here now, on this cold winter day, wrapped up in our warm coats and strolling around the almost deserted streets. I can only imagine how crowded it must be in the height of summer.

It's nearly 8pm and I'm writing my evening pages at Helen's home after forgetting to do them this morning. Billy and Owen are playing games, Helen is out with Merlin, and I have a night of rest and relaxation.

Book writing or *In Treatment*? Which shall it be? *In Treatment* followed by sleep wins. It's Saturday night, after all.

Sunday 12 December
Aix

"Courage doesn't always roar. Sometimes courage is that quiet voice at the end of the day saying, 'I will try again tomorrow.'" – *Mary Anne Radmacher*

The new day dawns. I don't write my morning pages. Helen drives us home. Billy hangs out with Owen all day. I still have a cold and I'm sullen and unhappy. I have no idea why. I try not to over-analyse it or judge it. I know it will pass. I try to write without much success. The day ends unsatisfactorily. Tomorrow is another day.

The Beginning of the End

Monday 13 December
Aix

"To be meek, patient, tactful, moderate, honourable, brave is not to be either manly or womanly; it is to be humane." – Jane Harrison

The morning pages are filled with more happiness and anticipation today.

It's only one week before Billy leaves. He's starting to get sad but he's also very excited about going home. I am too, actually. I'm starting to feel ready to settle into a new life in Melbourne, to create my new livelihood, buy a new home and continue to pursue an artistic life. But I have one big goal to achieve before then.

I write with pleasure and purpose all day until Billy comes home for his feast. As I attempt to leave to meet Loic for a drink, he stops me at the door.

"Where are you going, Mum? Do you have a date with François?"

"No," I say, with mock astonishment. "And who is François?"

He laughs. "Mum, you can't keep secrets from me. I know you had a date with François. Who is it this time?"

There's nothing this kid doesn't know.

"Okay, yes I'm going on a date. His name is Loic," I admit sheepishly, like some 16-year-old schoolgirl.

I'm totally amused by the role reversal as I walk down Rue Beddarides through Place des Augustins and down to La Rotonde.

I recognise Loic instantly as I enter. He's sitting up the back in a booth. My palms start to sweat and my stomach is a little queasy. He stands to greet me.

Right away he makes me feel relaxed and I order a Champagne to help the process along a little.

Loic is lovely. He's entertaining, and interesting and has even been to Melbourne. He shows me photos of his house, his family and his horses. He asks me questions about my time here and what I've been doing and we talk a bit more personally about our Meetic experiences.

I can tell he has really strong values. I really like him and I'm quite attracted to him too. After two very nice hours together, I thank him for the date, give him a little peck on the cheek and take my leave.

Less than two hours later I receive an email from him with the subject header 'Feeling'.

'I really spent a good moment with you,' it said. 'Are we going to meet again before your departure? I would like! Kisses Loic.'

Okay, so clearly he's keen to see me again. Yes, he was nice, and yes, I was slightly attracted to him and yes, it might be nice to go out with him again.

Then the 'buts' take over. But, I'm leaving in just over two weeks. But, I'm still getting over James. But, I'm still enjoying this love affair with myself. But, I have a project to finish and

The Beginning of the End

I don't need the distraction.

Then I wonder if I've just totally lost interest in men. Hell, I hope not!

I think deeply about what is right for me right now and soon a familiar sign appears: 'Wrong time. Wrong place.'

I do the honourable and honest thing and respond with, 'Dear Loic, It was lovely to meet you too. You're a very nice man, but I've decided not to pursue things further. I hope you understand. Cheers Carolyn'

Later in bed, I think about the patterns of my past and my behaviour with men and acknowledge that I've not always been honourable and honest. I decide that it's finally time to turn over a brand new leaf on that front.

Tuesday 14 December
Aix

"Like all of us in this storm between birth and death, I can wreak no great changes on the world, only small changes for the better, I hope, in the lives of those I love." – Dean Koontz

No huge revelations in my morning pages today. I'd better think of a more interesting topic to explore tomorrow.

Billy leaves for school and I check my emails. There's one from Julie in response to an email I'd sent with a few opening excerpts from the book. I'm nervous as I open it. What if she thinks it's a load of crap?

"I'm so excited for you, what a great read, you have truly done a magnificent job and I love how you're coming from such a feeling of space and being so willing to be authentic. It really kept me engaged! I'm so proud of you and inspired by you – gosh how your life has changed. You're a brave and amazing woman, and I know many women will relate to what you share in so many ways. Love Jewels."

It's wonderful to get such generous words of support, yet while it's lovely to have external validation, I'm aware that the most important validation must come from within.

The Beginning of the End

I still can't shake this pesky cold but there's no way I'm missing my very last yoga session with the elegant Elise.

In my usual corner at the yoga studio, I try not to breathe too excessively. I don't want to pass on my germs, although it appears I'm not the only one in the room suffering.

We move into the 'downward dog' pose and I check out just how close my heels are to the floor. They're much closer than they were three months ago, that's for sure. I've made good progress and I certainly feel more limber and light. We end with a handstand or two. It's fun, but I'm not sure how helpful it's going to be for this cold.

I bid farewell to Elise, thank her for her fabulous lessons and tell her they've been a significant contribution to my healing and that they'll be fondly recalled in my book.

So many wonderful things are coming to an end. Sadness creeps in for a while as I stroll back through the narrow, cobble-stoned streets of Aix towards home. Lately my feelings have been swinging from real sadness about what I'm about to lose forever and real excitement over what I'm about to discover in Melbourne.

Then, just for something different, when I arrive home, I write for the rest of the day. Cold or no cold, this book is going to be birthed. It's like a baby gestating. It's a baby girl, of course. She'll be born on 1.1.11 and while she may not make a public appearance for quite some time, there'll be no going back into the comfort of my womb once the last word is written. Scared? Bloody hell, yes!

Wednesday 15 December

Aix

"Disappointments are to the soul what the thunderstorm is to the air." – *Friedrich von Schiller*

Although Billy's 13th birthday is on Saturday, we've decided to celebrate it tonight, as most of his friends will have departed for the Christmas holidays on Friday. The plan is for an after-school party at home, dinner out and a sleepover with his five best mates. I've bought party snacks and decorations, booked the restaurant, borrowed all the sleeping gear again and organised a birthday cake.

I'm out on a very light run when Billy calls.

"Mum. Call the school. The three boys from the boarding house have been banned from leaving because they disobeyed some rules. They're not allowed to come to the party and sleep over. If they can't come I'm cancelling the whole thing."

At home I ring and even email the school to see if Billy's sleep over party can be salvaged. Nil response.

It's 1.30pm, the time they're all meant to be on the bus on their way into Aix, when Billy rings again.

"Mum, the boys definitely can't come. I'm cancelling the party."

When he arrives home, he plonks himself on the couch

The Beginning of the End

beside me for a hug. He's bitterly disappointed and sheds a few tears.

Later after Billy's feeling better, we decide to still have a party, one that's much more subdued. It's a relaxed and lovely dinner with Helen, Chiara, Owen and Merlin at the Korean BBQ place that Billy loves.

At home on our own, we top off the chocolate birthday cake with a hot chocolate before drifting off to sleep. In the face of such bitter disappointment, chocolate is Billy's only consolation.

Thursday 16 December
Aix

"Mothers of teenagers know why animals eat their young." – Unknown

Today I officially feel like crap. My cold has finally got the better of me. My nose and eyes are running like a tap so I reluctantly cancel my lunch with Nathalie, our French teacher.

I manage to write until midday when I look up to see my bed covered in tissues. Hmmm. Not pretty.

And as for the words I've written? I'm not concerned about the quantity, it's the quality I'm highly dubious about. I give it up and sleep all afternoon.

It's 5pm and Billy will be home soon. I can't be a rotten mum and just stay in bed. I haul myself out, aching all over, and take a shower, then go down to the supermarché to buy something for dinner.

With zero interest in eating myself, I simply grab the first thing I come across – hotdogs, baguettes and a bottle of sauce.

While the hotdogs bubble away in boiling water my unsympathetic son, who has somewhere along the line become a food snob, says, "Mum, your standards are really slipping."

I'm tempted to tell him where to go, but hold my tongue – only because I just don't have the energy to respond.

As he consumes two hotdogs smothered in sauce in about three seconds flat he says, "Actually, they're really, really good. Got any more?"

⚜ ⚜ ⚜

Friday 17 December
Aix

"Friendship is the only cement that will ever hold the world together." – *Woodrow Wilson*

The Beginning of the End

It's Billy's last day at school and he heads off for the bus with mixed feelings. The parents are invited for a lunchtime Christmas party with carols, mulled wine and nibbles. When I arrive, Billy is off having a last-minute muck up with his friends, so I take myself on a little tour for one last look around the school – the tennis courts, the swimming pool, the library where I'd held my book talks and the box-like classrooms where my son was taught.

There's been a downside to being in France for Billy. He's not done well academically and he's not had the opportunity to pursue any of his sporting or artistic interests. He's missed his dad and step-mum terribly and, of course, we've had some highly charged mother and son moments.

But the positives have far outweighed the negatives. Being here has given him an education in life and a broader appreciation of the world and the opportunities available to him. He's been introduced to a more liberal way of life in this co-ed school with no uniforms, and where the kids are mature and worldly. He's set the scene to do well at French for the rest of his school years. He's made great friends with many boys and, of course, just as many girls, from all corners of the world, and he's had his first real girlfriend here.

It's hard to believe that just 12 months ago he was finishing primary school at Claremont College in Coogee. Since then he's started high school at Scots College in Sydney, been to IBS in Aix en Provence, and soon he'll start at a new school, Melbourne Grammar, in a new city, Melbourne.

He's had some wild curve balls thrown at him in the last 12 months and he's swung his bat at all of them as best he could. Some he's hit for a six and others he's missed completely. He's given it all a go and for this reason alone, I'm very proud of him.

I could have continued to live the life we were living in Sydney and not chosen to turn his life upside down. I could have attempted to shield him from the uncertainty that accompanies drastic change and wrapped him up in cotton wool. I could have done a lot of things differently, that's for sure, but I have not one single regret.

As a result of this upheaval he's become more accepting, more social, more resilient, more worldly and more confident. It's changed his life and the lens through which he views the world.

It's time to for us to leave.

"Mum," he says stoically, "I'm really going to miss all my friends. I feel really sad and I want to cry, but I can't."

"That's okay," I say. "It's good to be sad. It means your time here will never be forgotten. Maybe you'll have a little cry later."

The Beginning of the End

Saturday 18 December
Aix, Billy's Birthday

"Between the innocence of babyhood and the dignity of manhood, we find a delightful creature of a boy." – *Author unknown*

"Happy 13th birthday Billy! You're now officially a teenager!"

I'm crawling up to his loft to give him a kiss and wake him up. It's 9am and he has a small window of time in which his father, family and friends want to Skype him and say happy birthday.

I hand him his card, a hot chocolate and some toast, and leave him to Skype for a while.

Some time later we head out for his final taste test tour of the markets, a Croque Madame at Les Deux Garçons and some birthday gift shopping. We visit the numerous, and by now quite familiar beggars to distribute all the small change we've been collecting and then buy his last ever citron meringue pie and baguette from Pauls. We return home via the same route he'd followed to the bus station every day, around the rotunda, up Rue de Beddarides and past the Hotel de Ville.

Although I try to jolly Billy along all day, it's a bit of a melancholy birthday to be honest, and I can tell he's really sad to be leaving. I can see it in his eyes every time I snap off a photo of him and in the way he hangs his head and frequently stares off into space.

It's a very subdued dinner at Le Passage, a very traditional French restaurant, and neither of us appear to be getting into the food. At times we reminisce about the various events that have occurred over the last four months and at other times a deep silence settles over us both.

At home he gives me a big hug. "Mum, thank you very much for bringing me to France. It's been the most fantastic experience and I'll never forget it."

⚜ ⚜ ⚜

Sunday 19 December
Aix to Paris

"Every new beginning comes from some other beginning's end." – *Jim Rohn*

The end is nigh. Today I'm taking Billy back to Paris so he can return to Melbourne tomorrow, while I'll be returning to Aix for my final 10 days of solitude and creativity.

The afternoon on the TGV is spent in silence. As we

The Beginning of the End

approach Paris, the snow is getting thicker and thicker and the chaos it's causing becomes increasingly apparent. The traffic on the way to the airport hotel has been reduced to a crawl.

After an average and uneventful dinner, we watch a little TV together while the snow continues to fall steadily outside and we drift off to sleep.

Monday 20 December

Paris

"We're born alone. We live alone. We die alone. Only through our love and friendships can we create the illusion for the moment that we're not alone."
– Orson Welles

We awake the next morning to a thick blanket of snow. I've no idea if we can get to the airport or if Billy's flight will even be leaving. With Gatwick and Heathrow closed and Charles de Gaulle at risk of closing, he might not get home.

The big buses that usually do hotel runs to the airport aren't operating so we're obliged to take a minibus that takes ages to arrive. The cars are skidding and sliding all over the road and at one stage our driver gets out to help push a car that's caught in a snowdrift in front of us. Finally we actually make it to the airport. First hurdle over.

The next hurdle will be to get through the check-in queue in time. Miraculously the queue is short and we're checked-in with 15 minutes to spare before Billy is to be collected as an 'unaccompanied minor' by the Singapore Airlines flight attendant. Second hurdle jumped.

The third hurdle? Will the plane even depart?

We look up at the board with the list of the departing flights. Most of them appear to be hugely delayed and many have been cancelled. As we prepare to say goodbye, I'm told I can't leave the airport until Billy's plane has taken off.

"It might be a long day and you may even see me again," I tell Billy. He doesn't seem worried or excited, just resigned to whatever happens.

It's time to go.

"I'll see you in three weeks. Thanks mate, for coming on this journey with me. I love you very much."

In an airport full of strangers he's not worried about showing his affection for me. He hugs me like a teddy bear, gives me a big squeeze and a kiss on both checks.

"Au revoir, Mum. I love you." Then he's gone.

An hour and a half later the flight finally takes off, and two hours after that my train leaves to take me back to Aix. When I finally arrive back at the apartment it feels cold and empty. I retreat to my bed, pull the covers over my head and accept loneliness as my friend until I drift into a restless sleep.

The Beginning of the End

Tuesday 21 December

Aix

> "A mother who is really a mother, is never free."
> – Honore de Balzac

I'm exhausted this morning. I didn't sleep at all well. I was worried about Billy all night, hoping he was okay on the plane on his own, and if he'll make it through Singapore airport to his Melbourne flight. Irrational perhaps, as he'll be accompanied the whole way. I'm also really sad about him leaving.

I fill a page of my journal with motherly worries, then choose another topic – my livelihood. I write for a couple of pages on this and finish up.

All I know is that I want to write more books and work on projects that empower women and help people build businesses that make a difference in the world. Other than that, it's as clear as mud!

This morning I have another phone conversation with Jane from Fitted for Work. We seem to be getting closer to a way we might work together. I'm still trying not to get attached to it, but I feel excited at the prospect.

I attempt a run around Parc de La Torse but I'm still not that well, so it's a short one. After getting myself a funky new

French hairdo, I stock up at the markets so I can bunker down and write.

That's when I receive a text from Billy's father confirming he's home safe and sound. Now there are no distractions and no excuses. My mind is 100 per cent clear and free to write. And that's what I do for the rest of the day. And the more I write, the closer I feel to victory.

Wednesday 22 December
Aix

"A community needs a soul if it is going to become a true home for human beings. You, the people, must give it this soul." – *Pope John Paul II*

After watching a couple of episodes of *In Treatment* last night, I can't help but write about it again this morning.

Why do I love that show so much? It's like a long series of lessons on how to connect and communicate authentically with others. I love it. Perhaps I should have been a counsellor or a therapist. What am I talking about? It's what I've been doing 'unofficially' for the last nine years since being in business. I can

The Beginning of the End

certainly continue to use these skills in my new livelihood next year.

I'm attempting another run this morning via a pit stop at Café des PTT to meet Helen and her husband Enrico, who has just arrived from China. I fully intend to just have a coffee to get my motor running, but before I know it I'm drinking Kir (a French cocktail of blackcurrant liqueur and white wine) with courtesy of Luciano, the owner of the café and a man I'd met at Richie and Agnés' party.

He tells me in broken Frenglish, that he's been reading our blog and that he's really enjoyed it, and he asks how Billy is. It's a small world. Aix really is just a big village with a vibrant, soulful community feel to it. It reminds me of my old café community in Coogee, just without the ocean and the surf club.

So after two glasses of Kir and a cough that conveniently decides to erupt again, the run gets postponed, date TBA. I bid au revoir and sprint home to make myself a healthy salad and settle down to write while I listen to Lucy Schwartz.

I'm singing out loud – "I want the sky to open wide, illuminate this fire inside" – and I feel deliriously happy. Maybe it's the Kir or maybe it's the delicious prospect of being able to write all afternoon. Does it matter?

Tonight's entertainment is a vin et fromage soirée at Domaine Les Bastides in Le Puy-Sainte-Réparade of the Bouches-du-Rhone, courtesy of Carole, a friend of Richie and Agnés'.

We start with a tour of the winery and a commentary on the winemaking process before the cheeses from all corners of France appear and the wine starts flowing.

A couple of glasses fuel my courage as I attempt to speak in French. I'm still very, very bad at it, but at least it provides my companions with some free and humorous entertainment for the evening. While I'd been anticipating that I'd be home by about 9pm for a couple of hours of writing before bed, it's 11pm when I finally roll in the door. Of course I'm in no state to write.

Thursday 23 December
AIX

"There's nothing to writing. All you do is sit down at a typewriter and open a vein." – *Walter Wellesley 'Red' Smith*

No raves and rants this morning.

It was a lovely night last night. This cold is still lurking. I'm going to sip honey and lemon drinks all day while I write.

And on it goes like this for about three pages. Boring words, boring sentences, boring morning pages, but kind of comforting really.

The fridge is stocked, the coffee is brewing, my artist's retreat is warm and cosy, the music is playing, my computer is fired up, and my brain and fingers are flying into action. I write

The Beginning of the End

with focus all day. The finishing line is well within sight, with the only competitors being Christmas Day and New Year's Eve. Will my social engagements beat me in this race?

Friday 24 December
Aix

> "Tis better to have loved and lost, than never to have loved at all." – *Saint Augustine*

The morning pages help me make sense of a very weird night.
It was a very strange evening in bed. I was extremely restless. I couldn't sleep and I couldn't stop thinking about James. It was so surreal. I wasn't dreaming. I felt like he was right beside me in this bed right here. Then I burst into huge, heaving sobs and I couldn't stop. And when I did stop, I just felt calm.

Only yesterday I'd booked flights to Sydney to see our friends for a week before Billy goes back to school in Melbourne. We're doing a house swap with Mick and Maureen. They'll be staying in our new home in Melbourne, and we'll be staying at theirs in Maroubra (just one suburb away from Coogee) and looking after Dash – which we're thrilled about. I wonder if that's the cause of my bad night? In just three weeks I'll be back in Sydney – so close, yet so far from James.

This man has been the source of my deepest pleasure and my deepest pain, yet I do not regret his presence in my life for one single moment. It's taught me so much about myself. I did not consciously choose to love this man. It happened almost without my consent.

Was the cause of my sobbing, fear or sadness? Maybe it was from fear that I've just been on the run since I made the decision to leave Sydney – that when I return to Australia, the pain may just come back with a vengeance. Or maybe it was from overwhelming sadness at the total and utter acceptance that he's out of my life forever and that I'll never see him again.

I truly don't know the answer, so I close my eyes for a minute and ask my Higher Power to take care of it for me. I ask her to fuel my faith that it will all be okay and that I'll attract a good, strong, available man into my life when the time is right.

It's 10am before I sit down at my little red writing desk in front of my computer, find a vein to tap and open it wide to let the words pour out.

Before I know it, it's Christmas Eve dinner – a lovely seafood affair with Florence and Marc at her home in St Marc Jaumegarde. We enjoy oysters, prawns, mussels, sea snails, crab and shrimps, with Champagne and conversation in a curious mix of English, Frenglish and French.

I should be revelling in this glorious experience in France but try as I might, I'm distracted and not fully present. I'm

The Beginning of the End

tired from last night's lack of sleep and I have a book to finish.

It's 2am before I arrive home and Skype Billy. It's Christmas morning there. He gives me a rundown on the booty he's acquired for his birthday and Christmas. Lucky kid!

He's really loving being home with his father and seems really, really happy. We blow each other a Merry Christmas kiss. I'm too exhausted to feel too sad and I fall asleep as soon as my head hits the pillow.

⚜ ⚜ ⚜

Saturday 25 December
La Bastide-des-Jourdans, Christmas Day

"Practice random acts of kindness and senseless acts of beauty." – *Anne Herbert*

My alarm rings and my journal beckons.

I feel sad and flat today. I'm all alone and lonely on Christmas day in beautiful France. I'm sad that I'm not with my son and my family. Yet I'm lucky to have such kind people around me here in Aix, like Florence who I shared dinner with last night, and Helen who has very kindly invited me to share lunch with her family today.

It gets me contemplating the concept of kindness and how it really does have the power to heal the world.

I write about the small, practical acts of kindness I can show Billy, my family, my friends, my clients and even strangers. Acts like giving hugs, complimenting people, listening more and talking less, asking thoughtful questions, giving small gifts of appreciation, making donations to causes I believe in and giving away possessions I don't need to people who do.

I also write down many simple little ways that I can be kinder to myself when I return to Melbourne – things like taking more baths, meditating daily, continuing my morning pages, eating healthily, doing yoga and more. It's a long list and a brilliant, thought-provoking exercise.

Helen has shown such kindness in so many ways to Billy and I since we first met some months ago. And now she shows kindness for the three men in her life, and me, as we devour the most exquisite lunch – oysters, Moroccan-flavoured fish, duck with roast vegetables and triple chocolate cake. It's a very un-Australian Christmas lunch and a nice change to be having a hot lunch in cold weather. By 3pm we're all ready for an afternoon siesta.

There's not much interest in dinner after that huge lunch.

I go to bed in Helen's home, much happier than I awoke this morning, and even happier that Christmas is over for another year.

The Beginning of the End

Sunday 26 December
La Bastide-des-Jourdans

"I fell upon the thorns of prose. I bled."
— *Julia Cameron*

It's 7am and I'm alone in Helen's beautiful big house looking after two cats, two dogs and seven puppies for two days while they go to Italy. The home has exquisite views, a huge fireplace and, most importantly, a big deep bath.

Writing is my occupation today – an unpaid occupation, for now, anyway.

I stop for an hour to take my camera out on my artist's date. The colours of the Luberon are exquisite and the camera loves them. There's a luminous light in this region, much like the Chianti region of Italy.

On return home, I take up my occupation again. Dinner is forgotten. Writing is all the fuel I need.

Monday 27 December

LA BASTIDE-DES-JOURDANS

"I lived in solitude in the country and noticed how the monotony of a quiet life stimulates the creative mind." – *Albert Einstein*

I'm in a state of peace and solitude as I fill my morning pages.

I love being on my own. With no disrespect to my son, having these last days here totally on my own has been the perfect way to finish my time in France. I can get up when I like (if I choose to get up at all). I can eat when and what I like (or not at all). And I can do with my time whatever I choose to do (something or absolutely nothing). In Sydney, I'd keep busy even if I was graced with downtime while Billy was at his dad's. Keeping busy was a way to avoid feeling my feelings. I pray that I'll continue to seek more solitude on my return.

I'm sitting on the sofa gazing at the brilliant cobalt blue sky thinking about a conversation I'd had with a friend a few days ago.

"You've had such a great time in France and it's been like a dream," she'd pointed out. "Wait until you get back to reality. It'll really hit you."

It really bothered me, this conversation. Yes this time in France was a dream, but right here and right now, it is my

The Beginning of the End

reality. I created it and I will create whatever reality I choose to create both back in Melbourne and for the rest of my life for that matter.

I refuse to go back to a life of feeling stuck. I refuse to believe that this trip is just a once-in-a-lifetime experience. It will be the first of many sojourns – I absolutely know it!

The promise of a bath once I've written another thousand words keeps me motivated to write. That, and the triple chocolate cake left over from Christmas lunch.

When I do get to the bath, I realise just how much I've missed having one since being here. Many times, over many years, I've sought solace in the sanctuary of a bath. I fill it to the brim and add some ylang-ylang oil and sigh that special sigh that comes with sliding into warm water.

I lay back for a full 15 minutes with a face-mask on. Then I cleanse every part of my body with a cotton cloth. I don't scrub myself vigorously like you'd scrub a grubby kid – but gently, with self-love.

When I step from the bath I dry my body slowly and mindfully. As I nourish my skin from head to toe with coconut oil, I thank each part of my body for its service to me and for being so wonderfully co-operative since being here.

When I emerge from the bathroom, I feel like a goddess primed for countless more hours of writing.

Tuesday 28 December
Aix

"Freedom means the opportunity to be what we never thought we would be." – *Daniel Boorstein*

I have hundreds of photos of Billy and scenic shots from our time here, but virtually no photos of me. So Helen, who has returned from Italy, is dropping me back into Aix this morning to go on a photo shoot with me.

She shoots me over and over – at my desk, on the balcony overlooking the stunning rooftops of Aix, at the markets, at Les Deux Garçons, down Cours Mirabeau and at Book in Bar. At least now I have some proof that I was actually here – other than this book, that is.

Helen leaves and I meet Frédérique, a fellow marketer, for lunch. We'd hit it off instantly at Agnés and Richie's party and had agreed to catch up before I leave. Over a long lunch and a fun afternoon we talk about our profession, her business, our lives and our families.

"Why did you move to France?" she asks earnestly, seriously wanting to know the real story that I hadn't really told anyone.

"To get unstuck. I didn't like the life I was leading or who I was becoming. I was in a difficult financial situation. I was

The Beginning of the End

in an unhappy, destructive love affair. I was bored with my business and deeply dissatisfied with the marketing profession. I was finding it tough and lonely as a single mum after so many years on my own and I wanted to give Billy the opportunity for an international experience and more of his teenage years with his dad. I was feeling helpless and stuck. I had to escape."

We talk for what seems like ages, about my life and hers and the life of a number of women we both know, women with children, mostly. We agree there must be millions of women (many of them mothers) around the world who feel stuck and who are not living the life they'd dreamed of.

When I'm in bed, my conversation with Frédérique continues to play on my mind. Before flicking off the light to sleep I say a long prayer for all the women I know and the millions of women I don't, who may be feeling helpless and stuck in some way. I wish them freedom and love and happiness.

Wednesday 29 December
Aix

"There is a woman at the beginning of all great things." – *Alphonse de Lamartin*

It's 9am and I'm still in bed when I start writing. I only get up to do my teeth, eat, get coffee and stretch from time to time. I don't venture out all day. I finish at 11pm and turn the light out. Fourteen hours of non-stop writing. I'm so close I can taste victory. All power to me and power to women everywhere!

Thursday 30 December
Aix

"As we are creative beings, our lives are our work of art."
– *Julia Cameron*

The Beginning of the End

I'm torn. I want to write but I also want one final day of creativity here in Aix to reaffirm my intention to live a creatively expanded life at home. I know the book will get finished. I can write in the middle of the night if I need to. So a day of creative pursuit it will be.

I start with writing my morning pages in Brasserie de L'Horloge over a café crème while gazing over the farmers markets. Then I prepare a list of all the people I want to buy gifts for and take one last stroll through the markets to buy exquisite photos of Aix and Provence, some L'Occitane en Provence and all manner of 'Made in Provence' products, some antique postcards and three big rolls of brown paper and ribbon.

At home, I play Leslie Feist and sing out loud as I lovingly wrap each gift for each person that I love dearly. I carefully select a postcard and write a personalised message on the back before attaching it to their gift.

When I've finished, I pack all the gifts in the bag with pride. It feels like the start of my own personal kindness revolution. If I get home without paying for excess baggage, it'll be a miracle.

In no time, I'm striding up the hill with my camera to visit L'atelier de Cézanne, the place where the French post-impressionist artist and Aix's town idol would paint from 6am every morning until 5pm in the afternoon. Both Matisse and Picasso are claimed to have said 'Cézanne is the father of us all' and I can see why as I survey his paintings of objects, scenery and people. They're distinctive in every way.

I walk around his workshop and gaze at the objects he used every day; the vase of flowers, the pitcher of water, the basket filled with fruit, the hardwood palette with the faintest remains of paint and the easels that once bore his masterpieces. Since being in my own artist's retreat, pursuing my own creative passion, I have a little idea of how he must have felt every day pursuing his purpose with such passion.

On the way home I snap more photos and walk past Cathédrale Saint-Sauveur. The bells are ringing and there are people outside, heads bent and tears flowing, as a hearse bearing a coffin is about to leave for the cemetery. It's incredibly sad, this scene, and I can't help but shed a few tears for the grief-stricken family and friends, all strangers to me.

I take my leave and continue strolling around the laneways of Aix and drop into my favourite vintage clothing store and buy a really cool 1980s black leather jacket. I feel just like Chrissie Hynde. All I need is a guitar, a black kohl pencil and a bit of musical talent to match!

It's 5pm before I arrive home. I roll my sleeves up and plant myself firmly at my desk and write like I've never written before.

The Artist's Way beckons me from my bedside table as I slide into bed much later. This book has been my rock and the catalyst for helping me unleash my creativity in so many ways, not just through my writing. It's also helped me revive my waning spirituality, and my love for life… and myself.

Before opening it I say a little prayer and thank Julia Cameron for writing it and Emma, my friend and protégé in Sydney, for recommending it to me. Then I thank myself for having the diligence and the discipline to stick at it day and night. I'm proud of myself, not in an egotistical kind of way, but in a gentle and self-respecting way.

The Beginning of the End

Friday 31 December

Aix

"There is no way to be a perfect mother and a million ways to be a good one." – Jill Churchill

New Year's Eve in France! It's 9.30am and I meet Helen for un café and to get our hair washed and blow-dried. I'm really sad to say goodbye to this intelligent, clever and worldly woman. I've learnt a lot from observing her with her two lovely sons. She's a very, very good mother. She's not a perfect mother, and neither am I, but who is? And what kid would want a perfect mother, anyway?

We say our last goodbyes and I walk home with a little sadness in my step.

It's now midday and I have seven hours to all but finish this book before I get ready to go to a NYE party at Frédérique's. For inspiration I watch Chrissie Hynde singing Radiohead's 'Creep' on YouTube and then listen to Radiohead themselves.

I intend to finish this book tomorrow morning (after tonight's party) on 1.1.11, a most auspicious date and my last day in Aix.

But for now, I'm committed to completing my final creative contract to myself. I reread the original contract I first made with myself in early September. Did I stick to it? Hell, yes!

Now I need to make a commitment for the next 90 days. I write the contract in flowing cursive in my moleskine, committing myself to another 90 days of morning pages, creative writing and self-nurturing on my return to Melbourne, and a longer-term commitment to pursue my vision to live a more creative life.

Now it's time to start sorting out my belongings, packing my bags and getting ready for what promises to be a most memorable NYE party.

It's 10pm before Carole picks me up for the party. The night passes in a blur and it's 4.30am before I stumble bleary-eyed into the apartment.

♣ ♣ ♣

Saturday 1 January

Farewell Aix

"The most terrifying thing is to accept oneself completely." – *Carl Jung*

I sit up in bed to write my last morning pages in Aix and my first morning pages for the new year. I'm waiting for 11.11am before I start writing.

The Beginning of the End

It's 1.1.11 and 11.11am. It's my last day here in Aix en Provence. I've loved this place so much. It's been the best gift I've ever given myself, maybe in my whole life!

I've made the most gorgeous friends. I've recovered my creativity. I've given Billy an experience he'll remember for life. I've recovered from an addictive love affair and restored a fair degree of my dignity and self-esteem. I've become fit and healthy, mentally, physically, spiritually and emotionally. I've even written more than 68,000 words to finish this book, my personal diary from the day I made a decision in Sydney to get unstuck, 238 days ago, to right now.

To be honest, I feel pretty tired after not getting home until 4.30am this morning, but I don't care. I went to the most fabulous party in a 17th-century farmhouse at le Domaine du frére, hosted by Frédérique and her family. I've never felt more accepted and embraced by a bunch of strangers.

We danced. We drank vin rouge. We had deep and meaningful conversations in Frenglish about kids, their education, relationships, life and love. We connected.

I'll be back. I make this promise to myself right now. This book will get published and I'll be back here to do an author's talk at Book in Bar one day. J'adore Aix! J'adore my life!

Tonight is my last night in this gorgeous town that's been our home for exactly four months. I'm meeting Lucia for one last drink and having dinner with Florence. Then tomorrow at 8.11am I'm going to leave this beautiful place and take the train to Andorra for a week of skiing with Wendy – one of my most precious girlfriends from Australia. We've been through thick and thin together for over 30 years.

It's going to be a week of fun and frivolity and no computer and no writing, except for my morning pages, of course!

And then I'm flying back to Melbourne to start a whole new life with Billy.

I can't believe I'm here right now, at the end of the latest chapter of my life. I'm rather pleased it doesn't end with a clichéd love affair that has me living happily-ever-after with a hot French man; otherwise there'd be no sequel. It does end, however, with something much greater – a commitment to never get stuck again and the courage to take on life's next great adventure.

The End

Epilogue

18 November 2013

UBUD & MELBOURNE

"Owning our story can be hard but not nearly as difficult as spending our lives running from it. Embracing our vulnerabilities is risky but not nearly as dangerous as giving up on love and belonging and joy – the experiences that make us the most vulnerable. Only when we are brave enough to explore the darkness will we discover the infinite power of our light." – Brené Brown

So now here I am in Ubud, Bali, writing this epilogue, almost three years since I got unstuck in Provence. (Hell, it really is starting to read like *Eat Pray Love*, sorry.) I'm at the end of a month-long working vacation and have just celebrated my 50th birthday while Billy (who's almost 16) has just returned from a three-week trek to the top of Mount Kosciuszko, the highest mountain in Australia.

When we returned to Melbourne in 2011, Billy started a new school, settled into his new homes and quickly adapted to spending half his time with his father and step-mum. I went to work at Fitted for Work (a not-for-profit helping women) and I resurrected my old business. I bought and renovated a

Epilogue

home (right near those beautiful Prahran Markets), continued my healthy lifestyle, made lots of new friends and enjoyed the rich and diverse culture of this wonderful city.

In 2012 and 2013, I continued on my life reinvention journey. I left the not-for-profit, became involved in Conscious Capitalism, started working at an amazing co-worker space called the Hub and have steadily reinvented my business from the ground up.

And Dash? Maureen and Mick unbelievably moved to Anglesea on the Great Ocean Road just an hour or so from Melbourne. So he is back in our lives and we get to look after him regularly when they go on holidays. Oh what a happy ending on that front!

And James? Crazily, after two years with no word from him and two brief and unsuitable relationships, I mustered up the courage to contact him. I was curious to see whether he'd changed and to know if I was totally cured of him.

It took an intense weekend with him in Melbourne for me to finally and completely understand that he hadn't changed and I wasn't cured.

Clearly my higher power had a plan for me. She wanted me to reacquaint myself with him so that I could finally deal with my malady around men and relationships and get the help I needed. I've not seen James for a year now and he's out of my life completely.

Throughout all this time, the morning pages have been my constant companion and my higher power has dropped more and more into my daily life. They've been the linchpin behind an amazing three years and helped me maintain the sense of freedom, dignity and self-respect that I found in Provence.

Unstuck in Provence remained a Word document buried in the bowels of my computer for a long time. Many times I'd announce to family and friends that I was going to publish it, only to be distracted by some other project or fun to be had. Yet I know the real reason that it remained unpublished was fear. I lacked the courage to put the intimate details of my life (and Billy's) up for scrutiny and I wasn't sure that my son should know about the finer details of his mother's indiscretions and insecurities. I also wasn't sure if he had the maturity to deal with his own story being in the public domain.

Writing the book seemed positively easy compared to the hoops I'd have to jump through to actually publish it, ensuring along the way that all parties, including Billy's father, would be happy about it. Many times I considered simply sending it to the trash and forgetting that I'd ever written it.

Then one Sunday morning after months of frustration with myself, I printed out the manuscript and very tentatively knocked on Billy's bedroom door. With a knot in my stomach and a deep breath, I gave him the manuscript and explained that I'd like to publish the book.

"Would you please read my book and share your thoughts on it with me. I'd be happy to eliminate or change anything you're not comfortable with," I said.

Then one day, a few weeks after I'd given it to him, he came into my room and tossed the manuscript on my bed.

"Mum, it's brilliant. I've written my comments in pen and edited some of the bits I didn't like. You can't write things like OMG – only kids use those words. I reckon lots of mums will be inspired by our story. You should just publish it." And then he promptly left.

Epilogue

Since that day, I've been steadily editing and re-editing and refining it to the point that I find myself here right now. The affirmation I wrote on that yellow card in Provence is sitting on the desk in front of me now.

I, Carolyn Tate, am a brilliant and prolific writer and author. My creativity heals my readers and myself, and leads me to truth and love. I live and work globally while earning an excellent income from my writing.

And now as I write this last sentence or two, I'm thrilled that I can finally ship it and print it. Until now, I've been pretty much able to control the process, but now it's out of my hands and it's over to you.

Published in 2014 in Australia by Carolyn Tate

Text copyright © Carolyn Tate 2014
Book Production: OpenBook Creative
Cover Design: Chantilly Creative
Cover Photography: Julie Renouf
Portrait Photograph: David Nendel Photography

Carolyn Tate asserts her moral right to be identified as the author of this book.

All rights reserved.
No part of this publication may be reproduced, stored in a retrieval system or transmitted in any form or by any means electronic, mechanical, photocopying, recording or otherwise is without the prior written consent of the publisher. The only exception is by a reviewer, who may quote short excerpts in a review.

Australia Cataloguing-in-Publication entry
Author: Tate, Carolyn
Title: Unstuck in Provence: The courage to start over

9781925144086 (paperback)
9781925144093 (ebook : ePub)
9781925144109 (ebook : kindle)

Subjects: Tate, Carolyn - Diaries.
        Tate, Carolyn - Travel.
        Self-actualization (Psychology) in women.
        Self-realization in women.
        Women - Conduct of life
        Assertiveness in women.
        Provence (France) - Description and travel.

Editor: Lucy Tumanow-West

Dewey Number:! 158.108

Disclaimer: This is a memoir and travel diary, and my interpretation of actual events. The names of people have been changed, where required, for privacy reasons.

www.ingramcontent.com/pod-product-compliance
Lightning Source LLC
Chambersburg PA
CBHW031057080526
44587CB00011B/715